RELIGION FOR TODAY

Judaism for today

Angela Wood

OXFORD UNIVERSITY PRESS

About the series

We live in a world where there are people of many different religions. In many of our towns and cities Buddhists, Christians and Jews live alongside Muslims, Hindus and Sikhs. If you travel abroad, you will soon experience whole countries that have been shaped by religion.

We all have different ways of looking at things. It could be said that we all see the world through our own "spectacles". These spectacles are made up of our beliefs, opinions, attitudes and values. What is important to you might not be important to me.

Religious people see the world through their spectacles, which affects the way they see and live in the world. We can't understand someone else's worldview unless we look through their spectacles. The *Religion for Today* series helps you to do this by giving you the skills and knowledge to understand people with beliefs different from your own.

In learning about another religion you will also be given the chance to think about your own life. So you will not only learn about the religions you study, you will also learn from the religions.

Chris Wright, Series Editor

About this book

The Jewish people is about 4000 years old and today there are about fourteen million Jews, living in every part of the world. Being Jewish is partly *religious* – having certain beliefs and values, and performing certain rituals. It is also *cultural* – a feeling of belonging together, having a shared history and destiny, and expressing the important things of life through certain customs. It is also *political* – being part of a worldwide community that is centred on Jerusalem in the land of Israel, and feeling the importance of Jews living safely and peacefully. This book explores some of these aspects of Jewish life through traditional writings and through the words of modern Jews.

In this book, Rabbi Hugo Gryn "speaks" many times, in many ways. He was very glad to be a part of it and enjoyed reading the first draft when he was ill in the summer of 1996. The book was completed on the day he died.

Angela Wood

For Judith Ish-Horowicz and Rachel Ouseley, the sisters I never had

Practical notes

- Many of the words and names that Jews use are Hebrew. In English books about Judaism, Jewish terms are written with English letters and this is a guide to pronounce them. The Hebrew terms are explained where they first appear and you can also look them up in the Glossary on page 62.
- The Jewish Bible is made up of three parts: Torah (the first five books – the most important part), Neviim (Prophets) and Ketuvim (Writings). The name Jews use for their Bible is made up of the initials of these three parts: "TaNaKh". There are several references to the TaNaKh in this book. This is an example of a reference: Deuteronomy 30:11. Deuteronomy is the name of the book, 30 is the chapter number and 11 is the verse number.
- Some dates appear in this book. Jews have their own dating system but also use the more common dating system for everyday life. Instead of AD they use CE (Common Era) and instead of BC they use BCE (Before the Common Era).

Contents

ONE

Who is a Jew?

This unit is about the Jewish people's feelings of belonging – their identity and their sense of community.

1 *If you are not Jewish, when did you first hear about Jews? What impression did you have of Jews? Have you had different ideas of Jews since then? If you are Jewish, when did you first realise it? What feelings did you have at the time? Do your feelings about being Jewish change at any time?*

An important part of being Jewish is belonging to the Jewish people that stretches across the world and over thousands of years. For most Jews, this feeling is stronger than what they believe.

Jews joining together in a protest against the war in Bosnia.

Young Jewish women joining together for prayer at Keva Akiva, the tomb of Rabbi Akiva, Tiberias.

Jewish identity

A Jew is someone born of a Jewish mother – or who chooses to become Jewish. There are born Jews who hardly practise their religion but still "feel" Jewish. For most Jews, though, being Jewish is not just about being born but about living. Although Jewish life has changed through the centuries, the important things are part of a long tradition passed from generation to generation.

The Jewish people were first called "Hebrews" and spoke Hebrew. They were also known as the "children of Israel" because they were descended from Jacob. His name was changed to "Israel" which means "struggle with God".

Israel" is a good name for our people because we've struggled with God many times. Sometimes we've struggled against God, questioning and arguing. Sometimes we've struggled with God to make the world better and seeing ourselves as partners. We've always called our homeland "the land of Israel". Israel is the name of the modern Jewish State. [Levy]

One story (in Genesis 18:17–33) describes how Abraham, the ancestor of the Jewish people, bargains with God. It took place about 4000 years ago near the town of Sodom (at the southern tip of the Dead Sea). Abraham sensed that God was going to destroy the town because the people were behaving so badly. . . Abraham felt that there was good in every people and so he asked God not to destroy the town if there were fifty good people in it. God agreed. Then, bit by bit, Abraham "beat God down" to ten. But ten good people could not be found in the town and it disappeared without trace.

2 (a) *How does God respond to Abraham? What kind of relationship do God and Abraham have? What might this say about Jewish images of God?*

(b) *Talk or write about an occasion when you have become closer to someone through arguing with them.*

(c) *In what way might people today "struggle" with God?*

Jewish communities

Jews whose families come from northern and eastern Europe are "Ashkenazi" and those from southern Europe and the Middle East are "Sefardi". They have their own customs and pronounce Hebrew differently. Sefardi pronunciation is now more common than "Ashkenazi" and is used in Israel today. In this book, where Hebrew words are written in English, the Sefardi pronunciation is followed.

❝ My family is Ashkenazi and we use Ashkenazi pronunciation at home and in synagogue. At my Jewish school, I learn modern Hebrew with Sefardi pronunciation. So I use them both – sometimes in the same sentence or even in the same word! There's a name for mixed-up kids like me: "Ashkefardi"! ❞
[Michael]

Two of the 'Besht Tellers' singing a niggun, a song without words. They are named after The Baal Shem Tov, a famous story-teller who emphasised the joy of being Jewish.

God

At the heart of Jewish life, three strands are woven together: **God, Torah** (the teaching) and **Israel** (people and land). This unit is about the Jewish understanding of God.

> " I believe there's one God who doesn't have a body, can't be compared to anything and created everything. We can feel God's creativity in nature, in relationships and in many things that happen. We worship God through prayer, study and trying to live good lives. "
> [*Elka*]

One of the ways that this belief is expressed is through the art and architecture of a synagogue: there are symbols of Jewish life but no pictures or statues of God, or of any human beings.

 *Why do some people think it is wrong to create pictures or statues of God? Is describing God in words different from showing God as a picture or a statue?*

Holiness

> " God is holy, which means special, distinct, separate, quite different from anyone or anything else. Some of God's holiness can be felt in life. People can join in holiness and something can become holy when they make something very ordinary special.
> [*Rabbi Hugo Gryn*]

> Holiness isn't physical but it's about ideals and a way of making our world better. There's a spark of holiness in everyone. The line from the Torah [the most important part of the Jewish Bible] "Be holy for I the Lord your God am holy" says many things about God and us, and how the two are closely entwined. Holiness is also practical. It's not just about beautiful thoughts but about ways we can make our ideals real. "
> [*Ester, 13*]

 What might Ester mean by "a spark of holiness in everyone"? How can holiness be "practical" and how can people "make ideals real"?

Some "practical" ways of being holy are given in the Torah, in Leviticus 19. Read these three short passages in the Bible. Each one has some notes and questions after it.

▶ Leviticus 19: 9–10

"Gleanings" are the bits of crops left behind at the edges of a field or in the corners, after the crops have been harvested. How do people often feel if other people give them things they need? Is it better just to leave it for them to take?

▶ Leviticus 19: 14

Ester says, "Not cursing the deaf and not putting a stumbling block in front of the blind means that we shouldn't do someone harm or hurt their feelings – even when we wouldn't be found out." Is something only wrong if you get caught? Is doing it *worse* if you do not get caught?

▶ Leviticus 19: 17–18

"Neighbour" means anyone you meet. Do you agree that you should tell people off if they're doing something wrong? If you don't, are you as much to blame as they are?

3 (a) Design a poster, a T-shirt or a coffee mug with one of these ideas of practical holiness as a slogan.

(b) Show how a character in a book, film or soap opera is living one of these ideas out.

Maimonides lived in Spain in the twelfth century and had some very practical ideas about holiness. He had the idea of a "ladder of charity" with eight rungs which are shown in this ladder. (The captions have been jumbled up.)

4 (a) Match these phrases (A to H) to the steps of Maimonides' ladder.

A when someone gives before they have been asked

B when the receiver knows who has given but the giver does not know who has received

C when someone gives grudgingly

D when someone gives willingly but less than they could

E when the giver gives so that the receiver becomes independent and never has to rely on charity again

F when the giver knows who they are giving to but the receiver does not know who has given

G when someone gives only when they have been asked

H when the giver does not know who they are giving to and the receiver does not know who has given

(The pictures show the correct order of Maimonides' ladder. Check with page 64.)

(b) Choose one step and write a story, or create a short play, where someone behaves in that way. Ask others to guess which step it is about!

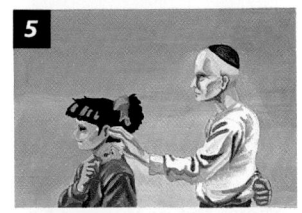

THREE

Torah

This unit is about the second strand: the Torah (Jewish teaching) which is given in the first five books of the Jewish Bible: Genesis, Exodus, Leviticus, Numbers and Deuteronomy.

> " Whatever is hateful to you, do not do to anyone else. That is the entire Torah.
> [*Hillel, a first-century rabbi*]
>
> It is a tree of life to all who grasp it and all who hold fast to it are happy. Its ways are ways of pleasantness and all its paths are peace.
> [*from the prayer book*]
>
> The teaching which I give you today... is very close to you, in your mouth and in your heart, to observe it. "
> [*Deuteronomy 30:11, 14*]

The beginnings of each of the Ten Sayings, in Hebrew, above the entrance of a synagogue in India. They appear in the form of the two stones of the covenant which the Torah says that Moses brought down from Mount Sinai.

Torah means "teaching" – all the things God has "told" the Jewish people – and it is the heart of their life. The Torah has stories about their early history, mitzvot (commandments) – things that they ought to do – and poems and sayings about life. It's divided into portions for each week of the year so that it is read in a never-ending cycle. The weekly portion is read in the synagogue on Shabbat (the Sabbath) and there are also special readings for festivals. Leah says: "We spend a lot of time studying the Torah but the Torah is to be lived – not just read and discussed. The Torah's about 'the good life' and a life lived by the Torah is full of goodness for other people."

Two particular festivals focus on the Torah: Shavuot and Simhat Torah.

Shavuot

Shavuot is the season of giving the Torah. It is also called the festival of Weeks.

There is a legend that when the Torah was revealed to the people through Moses on Mount Sinai, the mountain burst into flower, birds stopped singing and the whole universe was quiet and still – as if waiting for something wonderful. And the Torah itself tells what happened: there was thunder and lightning and a thick cloud, and everyone shuddered. God came down on the mountain in fire and it was full of smoke and then the *whole mountain* shuddered. Elka says, "*I* shudder whenever I hear that story – as we do on Shavuot which celebrates the giving of the Torah."

As well as mother's milk, the Torah is also compared to . . . a baby, a lamp, a coat, a comfortable bed, a glass of water . . . In groups, take each of these images in turn and brainstorm other words and phrases connected with them; for example, coat – warmth, protection from the weather . . . and so on. Then suggest other images which could express the meaning and the value of the Torah for Jews.

Some people have tried to find and claim Mount Sinai, and make it into a shrine. Alice says, "But the Torah warns us against even setting foot on it and we don't even know which mountain it was! Our tradition says that Sinai was in no one's land – so that nobody could say, 'You can't have the Torah: it's ours!' *and* nobody could say, 'We don't have to bother with the Torah because it's yours!' It was given for everyone, in all the languages of the world, in the wilderness."

 What are the good and bad points about being able to say exactly where something important happened – such as where someone fell in love or where a battle took place? How do people show that a place is important?

Simhat Torah

Simhat Torah – Rejoicing in Torah – is a festival at the end of Sukkot (see pages 12–13) just after the Jewish New Year. Over the year, the congregation reads the whole of the Torah and is ready to start again. On Simhat Torah, scrolls containing the Torah are paraded around the synagogue – usually at least seven times. A passage is read from the very end of the Torah, about Moses' death. Then another passage is read from the very beginning of the Torah, about creation.

At Simhat Torah in some congregations, the Torah is read under a tallit, looking like a wedding canopy, to symbolise the idea of Jews being 'married' to the Torah. There is a picture of a wedding canopy on page 40.

A favourite custom at Simhat Torah is to give out sweets or even throw them for people to catch and eat. Why do you think sweets are connected with Rejoicing in Torah?

FOUR

*I*srael

This unit is about the third strand: the people and the land of Israel.

Above: A bus stop sign in Jerusalem, in modern Hebrew script, Arabic and English.

Below: The Hebrew in the woman's prayer book and on the wall is in traditional script.

The people of Israel and their languages

 Do you and your friends have special names for things that no other groups have or perhaps do not even understand? Why do people sometimes do this and how does this make them feel?

Hebrew became the main language for study and prayer by Jews everywhere and that helps to unite them. Today it is the official language of the State of Israel. In daily life, Jews today speak the language of their country. In parts of Europe for centuries, Jews spoke "Yiddish". It is based on old German, with some words from other languages including Hebrew, and it is written in Hebrew script.

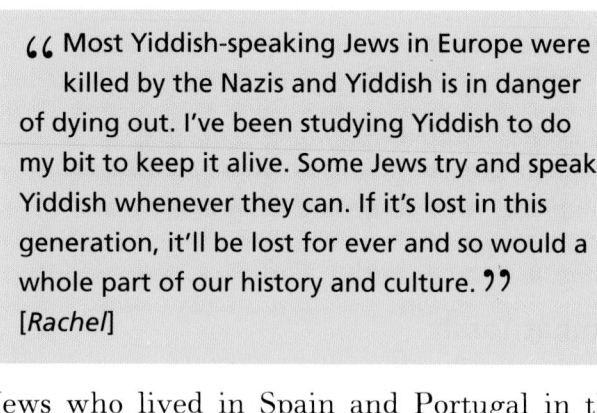

❝ Most Yiddish-speaking Jews in Europe were killed by the Nazis and Yiddish is in danger of dying out. I've been studying Yiddish to do my bit to keep it alive. Some Jews try and speak Yiddish whenever they can. If it's lost in this generation, it'll be lost for ever and so would a whole part of our history and culture. ❞
[*Rachel*]

Jews who lived in Spain and Portugal in the Middle Ages also had a special language, Ladino, which is like old Spanish. It, too, is hardly spoken now.

❝ When I first went to Israel, I couldn't speak Hebrew. The husband in the family I stayed with grew up in Romania where his family spoke Ladino. I'd speak to him in Spanish and he'd speak to me in Ladino – we understood each other! It was great for him because he seldom had a chance to speak Ladino and it was great for me because I could have a real conversation with an Israeli! ❞
[*Angela*]

The land of Israel

"The land of Israel will be small but the people of Israel will make it great."
[*Abba Hillel Silver*]

"For the Lord your God is bringing you into a good land . . . a land of wheat and barley, of vines and fig trees and pomegranates, a land of olive trees and honey."
[*Deuteronomy 8:7–8*]

"No matter where I go, it is always to Israel."
[*Nachman of Bratslav, 1722–1811*]

"We have a special feeling for the land of Israel and it's our homeland even if we live somewhere else. In the Torah, we read that God gave us the land to look after and live in. Israel's also the name for the whole Jewish people – not just those who live in the land. We feel that we're all related to each other and that whatever happens to *one* of us somehow happens to *all* of us. We have a saying, 'All Israel is responsible for each other.' So whenever Jews are together and united in spirit and action, there is 'Israel'."
[*Rafi*]

 Imagine you are on holiday in Israel. Look through this book and choose one of the photographs of Israel. Then write a message home about the place.

A painting in the home of Russian Jews who were not allowed by the Soviet government in the 1980s to go and live in Israel. The picture expressed their love and hope for Jerusalem and the flame that burned within them.

There is a story about an immigrant in Israel who passes an orange grove which looks very tempting. He leaps up on to the wall, grabs an orange and starts sucking its juice. A woman yells from the road, "Don't you know that it says in the Torah, 'You shall not steal'?" – "Where else in the world," he says to himself, "can you sit on a wall, on a lovely warm day, eat delicious oranges and listen to extracts from Scripture?"

 (a) What might the woman reply to the immigrant?
(b) What does this joke say about the Torah, the love of Israel and the value of humour?

"*The doorposts of your house*"

This unit is about ways in which the Jewish home is important, about the mezuzah (fixed to the doorposts) and the sukkah (a temporary home at the time of the autumn harvest).

"Hear O Israel, the Lord is our God, the Lord is one . . . Love the Lord your God with all your heart, all your soul and all your might. These words that I command you today shall be upon your heart . . . Write them on the doorposts of your home and at your gates." This mezuzah is on one of the gates to the Old City of Jerusalem which is like 'home' to the Jewish people.

1 *"Anger in the home is like rotten fruit," says the Talmud.*
"If you know you're going home, the journey is never too hard."
"You must go out into the world to know how lovely your home is."

Choose one of these sayings. Draw a picture to show what you think it means; or write a story, or create a role-play with one or more partners, where the saying is the punch-line.

The home is the most important place for Jewish life. It is where children learn about being Jewish, where the family can be sad or happy together. Especially in times and places where Jews have been persecuted, their homes have given them security and comfort.

The small box on the doorpost in the photograph is called a mezuzah. It contains the words of the "Shema", which means "Hear". The Shema is a prayer said in the evening and in the morning. Some of these words are in the caption. Having a mezuzah on the doorposts – both inside and out – reminds Jews that their home is Jewish, a place where God is worshipped, and that they live a life of Torah.

    ❝ The mezuzah is also like a badge for the Jewish home. I went to the Soviet Union a couple of times to visit Jews, take them things that they need and teach the adults and children. There was and still is a lot of antisemitism (persecution of Jews) there. I was amazed at how many Jews had a mezuzah on the front door because it identified them as Jews. I thought they were really brave – or stupid! But it meant a lot to them to say who they were! ❞
[*Angela*]

2 *What "badges" do other people sometimes put on the outside of their home to show what they believe in or value very much?*

A temporary home

Sukkot is the Jewish autumn festival. At that time, families and communities build a sukkah and live in it for just over a week.

> 66 A sukkah is a temporary home of natural materials. Ours has a wooden frame, with old blankets for walls. On the top, we've woven branches into a trellis, and hung fruit and vegetables inside. There's a gap in the roof to see the sky which sometimes lets rain in but does put us in touch with nature. It looks and smells beautiful and fresh. 99
> [*Ester, 13*]

Ṣukkot is a celebration of the senses – the fruits of the earth and of human hands. Elka says, "By building and living in a sukkah, we're also reliving the time when our ancestors wandered in the wilderness for forty years on their way to the land of Israel, and built temporary shelters as they went. We get a sense of what they went through and learn some of the same lessons from it."

A Jewish family that lives in a block of flats builds its sukkah on the balcony.

> 66 Human life is fragile and we're all vulnerable. The sukkah helps us feel that our strength comes from God and is inside us, that material things never last but love and faith never die. As the sukkah shakes in the wind and we wonder whether it will hold out, we're aware of people who are homeless but not from choice – and our heart goes out to them.
> [*Alice*]
>
> Sukkot is called "the season of our rejoicing". God commanded our ancestors and us, "Be happy!" I only half understand how you can *tell* someone to be happy! But I know that when you do happy things and make other people happy, you are in touch with the well of happiness inside you – and it works! 99
> [*Rabbi Hugo Gryn*]

3 (a) Read what Elka says. Why is it important to **relive** the story and not only tell it? What might they learn from it?
(b) Design a poster for a "Be happy!" campaign.

A woman tying foliage to the roof of a sukkah.

13

"*From generation to generation*"

This unit is about Jewish parents and children, and the festival of Passover – Pesah – in which children and parents play a big part.

One of the mitzvot in the Torah – in fact, one of the Ten Sayings (also known as the Ten Commandments) – is "Honour your father and mother" (Exodus 20:12 and Deuteronomy 5:16).

> ❝ There's no mitzvah the other way round – that is, saying "Honour or respect your children!" That's because parents naturally love and value their children but children don't naturally love and value their parents and they have to be commanded to! ❞
> [*Alice*]

 1 Do you agree with Alice that parents naturally love their children and that children do not naturally love their parents?

Each of the pictures shows a plague that struck Egypt when the Jews were slaves there. They came from a "haggadah", a medieval book illustrating the time of slavery.

> ❝ I really *feel* that it's Pesah because for a week I eat different things – matzah instead of ordinary bread, and no hametz at all. My whole digestive system seems to change! And we have crockery, cutlery and cooking utensils just for Pesah. There's no chance we wouldn't *know* it's Pesah! ❞
> [*Rabbi Hugo Gryn*]

Pesah – the festival of Passover

Pesah is the Jewish spring harvest festival but it celebrates other important events and experiences, too. One of its names is "the season of our freedom". It involves parents and children together in very special ways.

The ancient Jews were slaves in Egypt for 400 years, in the time of the pharaohs. They believe that they were only able to escape because God helped them and it is the most important experience in their history. The story is told in Exodus 12 and 13.

They had to leave at night, in a hurry, and did not have time to let their bread-dough rise as usual so they baked it as it was – and it turned out flat. It is called matzah, unleavened bread. Before Pesah, Jews eat up or clear away all their hametz (leavened foods), such as ordinary bread, cakes and biscuits.

On the first night of Pesah (and, for Orthodox Jews outside Israel, on the second night as well) there is a special supper with songs and stories and lots of time to talk: it is called a seder (which means "order"). At the seder, Jews read, sing from and discuss a book called a haggadah (which means "telling").

> 66 The seder is a meal and a play and a concert and a story and a party and a discussion – all rolled into one. There are lots of stories to be told, and songs to be sung and interesting things to do and eat – as well as a big tasty meal in the middle. 99
> [Joanna, 9]

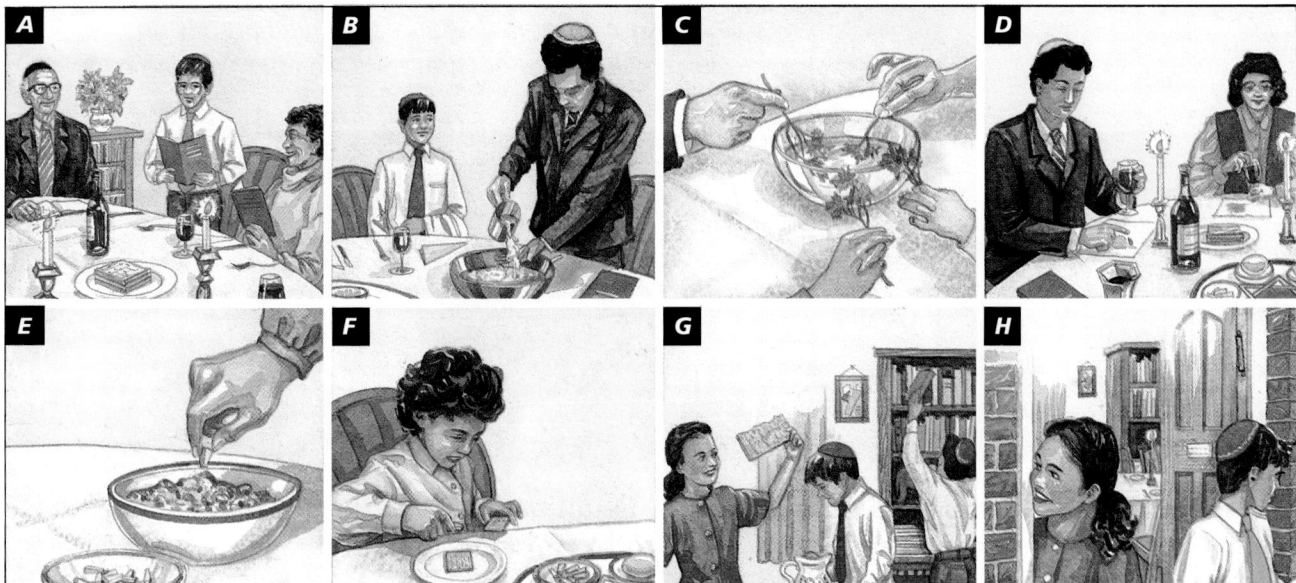

A child singing four questions

B washing hands

C dipping green vegetable in salt water/vinegar

D dipping fingers in wine and "flicking"

E dipping maror, a bitter vegetable, in haroset, a paste which resembles cement

F making a "Hillel" sandwich of matzah and maror

G children searching for/finding afikomen, the piece of matzah which is hidden during the first part of the seder and then found after the meal and eaten at the beginning of the second part of the seder

H opening the door for Elijah

 2 These are some of the themes of the seder. Look at the pictures of the seder and say which picture you think goes with which theme. (There may be more than one picture for each theme.)

a sweat and tears of slavery

b bitterness of slavery

c the bread of hardship

d the hope that the Messiah will come

e the joy of freedom

f springtime hope

g feeling sorry for those who suffered the plagues

h the sweetness of a good life

i stories, songs, questions and answers

(The answers are on page 64.)

*M*en and women

This unit is about the parts played by men and women in Jewish life.

1 Is it important to you that men and women do different things at home? Does it show that they are different? Should they deliberately do the same things – or swap over – to show that they are really the same?

▶ Look closely and talk about these pictures. What does it tell you about the various roles that Jewish men and women play in the home?

❝ Jewish men have to do all the mitzvot [commandments] but women sometimes have to do other important things that might make it impossible for them to do the mitzvot. For example, if a baby needs breast-feeding, the mother can't say, "Sorry, baby, I can't feed you – I'm going to do a mitzvah instead!" Jewish tradition says that breast-feeding the baby is *more* important than any mitzvah and only the mother can do it. ❞
[*Clive*]

Traditionally, Jewish men and women play different roles but each is important in running the home and raising children and each has their part to play in Jewish rituals. For example, for Shabbat (the Sabbath) and festivals, the woman bakes the bread and lights the candles, and the man sings the blessings for the day, with wine or grape juice, and breaks the bread.

In most congregations, men and women pray separately, and children can be either with the men or with the women. For congregational prayers, there is a minyan, which means a minimum of ten adult males. Men are expected to pray three times a day. In some congregations, men and women pray together and do not count a minyan.

In several places today, there are traditional women who feel excluded from congregational prayers and want to have a minyan of their own. Some have started meeting for prayer and study on Shabbat. The cartoon shown here takes a light-hearted view of this.

NOW DEAR, WHILE I'M IN SHUL - DON'T YOU AND THE BOYS MAKE A MESS AT YOUR COFFEE MORNING!

▶ What images of men and women are there in this cartoon?

Women in Jerusalem praying at the Western Wall, the last remaining wall of the ancient temple which was destroyed by the Romans in 70 CE. The space in front of the wall is divided into an area for men and an area for women.

▶ Why do you think it is important for some women to pray together?

> ❝ It feels good for women to pray together and it's allowed in our religion. We're not asking men to change what they do or give us parts to play in their services. We accept that men and women are different. But different can still mean equal! ❞
>
> [*Sara, a member of a woman's minyan*]

"My grandmother's kitchen"

Jewish mothers and often grandmothers play a special role in creating a Jewish home, in raising the children and in setting examples of Jewish values. Rabbi Lionel Blue was a child in the East End of London in the 1930s and remembers simple acts of kindness, done without fuss:

> ❝ My grandmother took me on expeditions. On Thursday nights she woke me up at dead of night . . . we went round the block, putting little packets through letter-boxes. They were little parcels of money and food to help poorer families celebrate the coming Sabbath. They were given at night so that giver and receiver would never meet, and neither would feel obligation or shame. Occasionally, we met other "bubbes" [grandmothers] wrapped in shawls and shadows waddling from house to house. ❞
>
> [From *A Taste of Heaven*]

 (a) Imagine the scene on Friday morning when members of a family find little packets of money. What would they make of it? Create a dialogue that might take place between them.

(b) Why should the giver and receiver not meet? Would the receiver like to know who had given the little packets?

"You are what you eat – and what you don't eat"

This unit is about the meaning of food in the Jewish tradition: what Jews do not eat – and why.

> 66 We say blessings at many times and there are blessings for various foods. God made everything and we didn't, so, with these blessings, we're really saying that God is blessed and we're thankful. That's how we make ordinary things special. 99
> [*Amit, 12*]

"Blessed are you, Lord our God, ruler of the universe who creates different kinds of food." These children at a Jewish school are saying blessings before their packed lunch.

1 *What might someone who was not Jewish say before eating to show that they were grateful for the food?*

2 *Are there things that other people eat that make you feel "funny" or go "Yuk!"? How do you explain that?*

There is no such thing as *Jewish* food! There are some foods that Jews especially like to eat, or are used to in the place that they live or their family came from, or that are special at particular times. But Jews eat many of the same *kinds* of food as other people. There are, though, certain foods that Jews do *not* eat and that is what makes the difference.

The "funny" feeling is a food taboo – something like a message inside us that tells us we should not eat this or that. Perhaps we get the taboo from our family or it is part of our culture. We all have food taboos and they're an important part of our identity. Jewish food laws and values are called "kashrut". The basics are given in the Torah and the ancient rabbis sort of spelled them out. "Keeping kasher" means that, several times a day, we remember who we are and what matters to us.
[*Alice*]

Kashrut

Food that Jews may eat is called "kasher" or "kosher" which means fit, proper or right. "Tref" is food which Jews may not eat: it means "torn" and comes from the idea of strangling an animal – which Jews are not allowed to do. Jews do not have to memorise long lists of foods: there is a simple formula for kasher food. Look at the table.

Plants All food and drink from vegetables, fruit and grains

 Meat From mammals that chew their cud and have split hooves, e.g. cow, sheep, goat

 Poultry From domestic birds that eat grain, e.g. chicken, duck, turkey

 Fish From fish that have both scales and fins, e.g. cod, mackerel, plaice

 Eggs From kasher birds

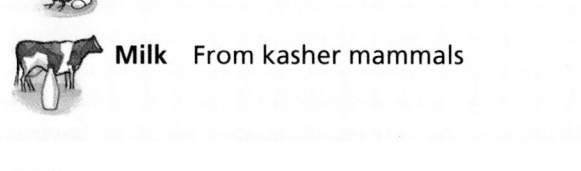 **Milk** From kasher mammals

These shop signs in London show that the food on sale is "kasher".

 3 *Sort these foods into kasher and tref:*
(a) *chocolate milkshake*
(b) *prawn cocktail*
(c) *cod and chips*
(d) *pork chops*
(e) *curried goat*
(The answers are on page 64.)

Milk, meat and "parev"

Jews believe that people should respect and care for animals. Religious Jews only eat meat from animals which have been slaughtered in the way that they think causes the *least* pain. They think it is cruel to shoot, trap, club or strangle an animal as it may take a long time to die in pain, and they do not eat meat from animals that have been killed like that. The Jewish method is quick. The slaughterer is specially chosen and trained, and must use a very fine, sharp knife so that it does not pull on the animal's skin. He finds a certain place in the animal's neck and makes one quick cut so that the animal dies straight away. Then he lets the blood from the animal drain away as it represents the life force of the animal and can return to the earth.

" One of the mitzvot in the Torah says that we shouldn't eat a kid that was stewed in its mother's milk. Maybe some people did that once and the Torah's saying it's wrong. The rabbis, about 2000 years ago, thought it had a deeper meaning, too. They said it's about protecting the feelings of the mother because she feels that her milk is for the life of her baby not for its death. The rabbis said this should hold true for all animals. So religious Jews don't cook or eat meat foods and milk foods together. Food that's neither meat nor milk – that's *most* food – is called "parve" or "parev" – like vegetables, fruit and grains, and kasher fish and eggs. Parve food can be eaten with meat, with milk or on its own. If it is eaten with meat, the dish becomes "meat"; if it is eaten with milk, the dish becomes "milk". It's not as complicated as it sounds! "
[Yoheved]

 4 *Draw up a menu of kasher food and drink for either a family picnic, a wedding reception, a supper at a youth camp or a child's birthday party.*

The best of days

" Willingly and with love he gives us his holy Shabbat to inherit, for it recalls the act of creation. This is the first day of holy gatherings, a reminder of the exodus from Egypt.
[*from the Shabbat kiddush*]

More than Israel has kept Shabbat, Shabbat has kept Israel. "
[*Ahad HaAm, 1856–1927*]

A painting by Philip Ratner, showing kiddush at a family table. The Hebrew word at the top says 'Shabbat'.

" It's a holy day, not like any other day of the week at all – it's brilliant. Jews who keep Shabbat holy don't do any work at all on Shabbat. We don't go out to work or to school, don't do any housework or homework. Instead we have a relaxing day, reading, eating, having a nap, going to synagogue and just hanging out together ... We look back on the last week and it fits us up for the next week. "
[*Tamar, 12*]

Jewish days start and end at sunset. Shabbat lasts from Friday evening to Saturday evening. Shabbat is the Hebrew name for the seventh day of the week. None of the other days has a name – just numbers: Sunday is the first day, and so on. But Shabbat has a name of its own because it is special, a holy day.

Observing and remembering

Joanna says: "Shabbat is partly about what we do and don't do, and partly about what we feel or don't feel." In one version of the Ten Sayings there is the commandment: "Observe the Shabbat and keep it holy," and in the other version it says, "Remember the Shabbat." Observing stands for *doing* and the outward signs of Shabbat. Remembering stands for *feeling* and the inner meaning of Shabbat. Shabbat is sometimes described as a queen who demands actions, and sometimes as a bride who inspires feelings. This Friday evening song of welcome for Shabbat expresses these ideas:

The sun on the treetops no longer is seen.
Come out, let us greet the Sabbath, the queen.
See! She descends, the holy, the blessed,
her messengers with her, of peace and of rest.
　　Welcome! welcome the queen!
　　Welcome! welcome the bride!
Peace be with you, messengers of peace!

1 *Design a bookmark, based on one or more lines of this song, for a book that a Jew might read on Shabbat.*

Work and rest

 2 (a) *What does "work" mean to you?*
(b) *List the things you do in a day under "work" and "rest" headings. Then compare your list and definition with someone else's.*

The rabbis found there were thirty-nine different kinds of actions which Jews should not do on Shabbat. They fall into five groups:

1 preparing food
2 making cloth
3 writing (which includes preparing the parchment – animal skin – to write on)
4 building
5 carrying something from private property to public property (or the other way) or in public property.

The rabbis said that anything that was *like* one of these actions also counts as work. All of these actions involve making or breaking something in a physical way. But Jews value life very highly and *anything* can and must be done on Shabbat to save someone's life.

3 *Decide which is these actions or activities counts as work, from the point of view of keeping Shabbat:*
a) *making a cake*
b) *reading a letter*
c) *moving a chair to your neighbour's house*
d) *driving an ambulance*
e) *writing a letter*
f) *eating cake.*

Check with page 64.

❝ The Torah says that Jews shouldn't make fire or travel very far on Shabbat but there is obviously more to work than that. The rabbis, about 2000 years ago, thought that work wasn't just a personal *feeling* but definite *actions* which everyone could accept. They felt it was important for all Jews to keep Shabbat in similar ways so that the community would be together. So they defined "work". ❞
[*Moshe*]

▶ *Match the five 'groups' of work to the actions in the picture.*

❝ We go to a lot of trouble to get ready for Shabbat. We shop for really nice food, do the cooking and cleaning, have a bath, wash our hair, put on clean clothes and lay the table. Everyone pitches in. We work very hard for Shabbat – and then we don't have to work at all! ❞
(*Abe*)

A day in the life of Shabbat

This unit is about the ways that Jews celebrate Shabbat and about the themes of Shabbat: God, Torah and Israel.

Shabbat is divided into three periods: Friday evening, Saturday morning and noon, and Saturday afternoon. There is a meal in each period and each of these has a different mood: Israel, Torah and God.

Friday evening

On Friday evening, the emphasis is on Israel – being together in a happy mood.

"This day for Israel is light and joy, a Shabbat for rest." (from a Shabbat song composed by Isaac Luria, 1534–72) The mother of the family lights candles at the start of Shabbat. There are always at least two: one for "observe" and one for "remember".

> ❝ We recite kiddush with wine or grape juice. "Kiddush" means "making holy" – because we're turning an ordinary drink into something special. It's not magic! It's still a drink and it tastes like a drink but something about it is different. Maybe it's changed because we've changed or maybe we've changed because it's changed. It's got the Shabbat flavour – and so have we! ❞
> [*David*]

> ❝ Some Jewish women light candles on their own but I love the family and friends all around. The candles cast a warm glow and there's a feeling of being together in peace and holiness. ❞
> [*Judith*]

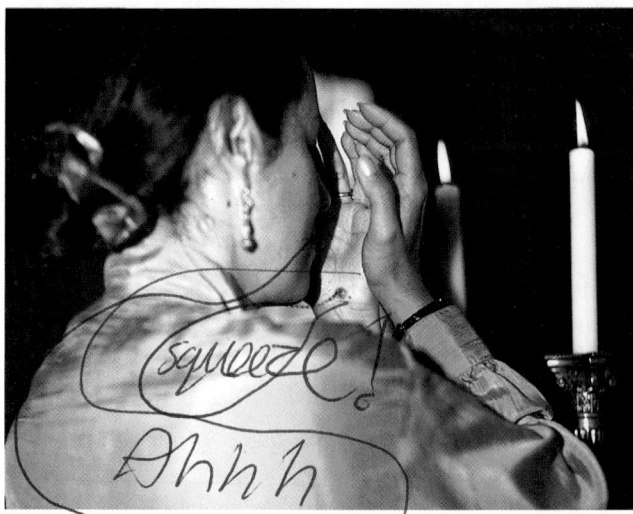

After lighting Shabbat candles, a Jewish woman covers her eyes as she says the blessing.

This Jewish father in London is reciting kiddush while lifting up a silver goblet.

> ❝ We sprinkle salt on the hallah because it takes a lot of work – er, sweat! – to make bread. Also because we're human: animals don't flavour their food – humans do. We never pass the bread from hand to hand because it comes from God not just through human effort. Where I come from, it's our custom to throw the bread to each other so it sort of comes to you from the sky! ❞
> [*Baruh, a Yemeni Jew*]

Saturday: morning, noon and afternoon

The main Torah reading of the week is on Saturday morning. The emphasis at lunch-time is on Torah – on discussing the weekly portion and studying together.

On Saturday afternoon, the emphasis is on the individual and God – a quiet time for private thoughts and close relationships. The late afternoon meal is light and simple.

After Shabbat

When Shabbat goes out, there is a short service called havdalah. It means separation, and is the time when Jews separate Shabbat from the week that is about to start. There are sweet spices in the spice box – such as cinnamon, cloves and nutmeg. The havdalah candle is plaited, like the hallah, with God, Torah and Israel coming together.

Children holding their hands to the light when making havdalah. These children at a Jewish school make havdalah on Monday mornings – as they return to 'work' together for the first time after Shabbat.

> ❝ We start with wine, then we take a big sniff of the spices because we want the lovely fragrance of Shabbat to come into the working week. We hold our hands up to the candle and see the shadows our fingers make on our palms and our nails go glowy. Then we put some wine on a plate and put the candle out in it. Lighting fire and putting fire out is work – and then we know for real that the week's work has started again! But one more thing ... we sing a song hoping that the Messiah will come. That'll be one day when everything is perfect ... We got a little taste – for just one day – of what the world could really be like and now it's over so we want it to come back and stay for ever! ❞
> [*Alice*]

1 *In what ways do you show that you do not want something to end or someone to leave?*

2 *Create a timeline for "a day in the life of Shabbat".*

3 *Choose one Shabbat picture (from pages 20–23) and describe its mood – without saying what is actually happening in the picture. Share your description with a partner or in a group and ask them to say which picture you have described.*

"A house of meeting"

This unit is about the synagogue as a community centre and meeting place, the physical layout of a synagogue and about the festival of Purim celebrated in synagogue.

> " You can take the Jew out of the synagogue but you can't take the synagogue out of the Jew! "
> [a Yiddish folk saying]

A synagogue is a Jewish community centre and is like a Jew's second home. Sometimes a community cannot afford a building of its own and members meet in each other's homes. Many synagogues begin like this. Most synagogues have several rooms which can be used for study, prayer and all sorts of meetings and social activities. Some have only one main space which is used for all activities.

> " My class sometimes visited places of worship of other religions. I could never understand why most of them had no toilet! We use synagogues for so many things, we're often there for hours and we usually have something to eat and drink – so a synagogue without a loo is unthinkable!
> [Clive]

> There's more to worship than prayer. Worship's about learning and discussing things together, or any activities to do with Jewish life. Worship's about just being together, too. You can't really be a Jew on your own. "
> [Rachel]

The word "synagogue" comes from Greek, and some North American and German Jews call it "temple". There are three Hebrew names and they mean: house of meeting, house of study and house of prayer. Each one says something about what the synagogue is for and how it is used. "House of meeting" is the name mostly used in Israel.

All synagogues have an ark, a cupboard containing the Torah scrolls, which is usually on the wall facing Jerusalem. Above the ark there is an "eternal light". Most synagogues have a raised platform called the "bimah". This is where the prayers are led and the Torah is read. Traditionally, the bimah faces the ark and is in the middle of the synagogue, with the congregation all around. In some modern synagogues, the bimah is right in front of the ark, facing the congregation. The position and direction of the bimah makes a difference to the congregation.

The mother of the bride hands her daughter the cup of wine, under the wedding canopy in a synagogue (see page 40).

1 *What difference do you think the position and the direction of the bimah makes to the reader or leader, and to the congregation?*

Purim

Purim is a minor festival which falls in February or March. It celebrates how Ester, a Jewish woman married to a king of ancient Persia, saved the Jewish people from destruction. An important part of the celebration is the reading of the Book of Ester in synagogue. Whenever the "baddy" in the story is mentioned, everyone tries to drown his name and the noise is deafening! Wearing fancy dress makes the whole occasion even more festive.

Children in fancy dress for the Megillah reading - and the party, plays and parade afterwards!

 2 *(a) Read the story of Ester from a Bible or a shortened version in another book.*
(b) How does the celebration of Purim come from the story?
(c) In the photograph of Purim, which aspect seems to be the most important: study, prayer or meeting?
(d) What does the festival of Purim say about Jews' attitude to the synagogue – and to the place of study, prayer and meeting in Jewish life?

Voluntary social work in the community and raising funds for charities are an important part of synagogue life. During World War II, a bomb that fell near West London Synagogue damaged the domed roof and destroyed the ornate ceiling. The congregation collected money to have them restored but then heard that young children on the Continent, whose families had been killed in the Holocaust, had no homes. They immediately decided to use the money to create a home for the children in Britain. The roof of the synagogue was made safe but with a plain ceiling. Elka, a member of the synagogue, says, "I think the plain ceiling is much more beautiful – in a different way. Whenever I look up, I remember the story of the children. It's a story of new life, a story of the bond between Jews across the world, a story about loving other people and loving God – a story of real worship."

 3 *What do you think Elka means by "real worship"? Look back at what Rachel says on page 24.*

"*A* house of study"

This unit is about the synagogue as a place of learning.

❝ It's more important to be a learning Jew than a learned Jew. ❞
[*Rabbi Hugo Gryn*]

1 (a) *What is the difference between learning and being learned?*
(b) *Is it more important for you to be learning than learned?*

2 *A Torah scroll is buried when it can no longer be used. In the photograph the Jewish girl is kissing her prayer book because she dropped it. What do these actions say about Jews' attitudes to their writings?*

Most synagogues are used for study more than for anything else. Services on Shabbat and festivals usually have a sermon given by the rabbi or another member of the congregation. Most synagogues have classes for children on Sunday morning, and sometimes after school as well. There are Shabbat study groups for different age groups to discuss the week's Torah reading and, throughout the week, all sorts of classes and activities – such as Hebrew or cooking. In Orthodox communities, men and women study separately; in Progressive congregations, they study together.

The heart of the Torah is the Ten Sayings (Commandments) and, to express their importance, they are clearly displayed in synagogues. (Look again at the photograph on page 8.)

3 (a) *Read the Ten Sayings in Exodus 20:3–17 and summarise them in your own words.*
(b) *Why do you think the Ten Sayings (or the first phrase of each one) are usually displayed on the walls of a synagogue or on or above the ark?*
(c) *Choose one of the Ten Sayings and discuss its meaning for today.*

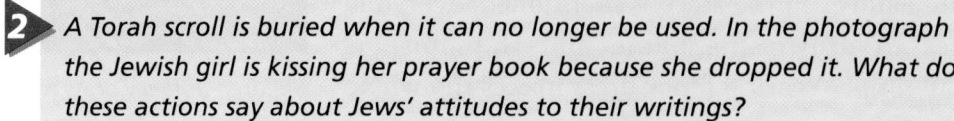

This girl dropped her prayer book. She now kisses it as a mark of respect.

Reading the Torah

The highlight of all Jewish study is the reading of the Torah from a scroll – always in a morning. Traditionally this takes place on Mondays and Thursdays, on Shabbat and on major festivals.

4 (a) These words are to do with the Torah and the way that it is used but the letters are jumbled up. Unscramble the letters to make the words: hrToa; rloscl; versli; llesb; uesgaogny; wbo; ngrfsei; ftlide; retinop; orwsd; emnthcpar; kra.

(b) Referring to the pictures, copy out the captions and fill in the blanks using the words you have made (the answers are on page 64):

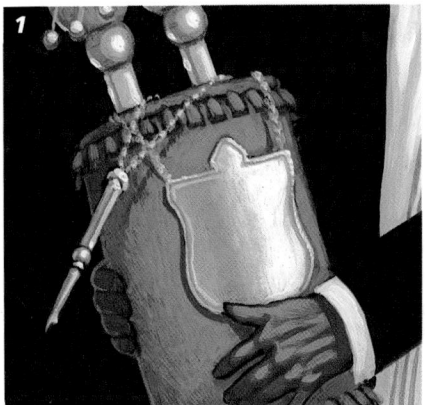

Each _____ _____ is covered in a decorative case or cloth, with a _____ plate and pointer hung around it, and silver _____ on top. It is taken from the ark and paraded around the _____.

As it passes, people often _____ to it or touch it with the fringes of their prayer shawl and then kiss the _____.

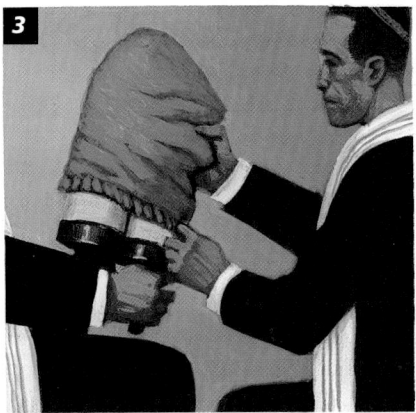

Someone takes the bells, the pointer, the plate and the cover off the _____ _____ and carries it to the reading desk.

The Torah is _____ in all directions so that everyone can see the text. In Sefardi congregations, this happens before the Torah is read. In Ashkenazi congregations, it is raised afterwards.

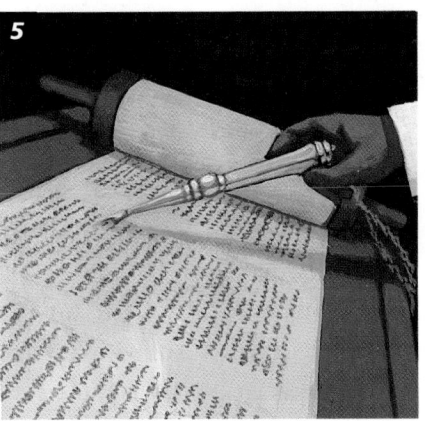

People who read from the _____ use a long _____ , called a yad, which means hand. This helps them follow the _____ , which are very close together, without smudging the _____ with their finger.

After the reading, the cover, the plate, the pointer and the bells are put back. The _____ _____ is paraded round the _____ in the other direction and put back in the _____.

5 (a) Why do you think the Torah is taken out, read and returned in this ceremonial way?

(b) Create a child's picture book, with simple captions, that a child could follow during the ceremony of the Torah reading.

"A house of prayer"

This unit is about the synagogue as a place of prayer.

> " The heavens above, the highest heavens, cannot contain you – how much less this house that I have built! "
> [*King Solomon, about 900 BCE, when the first temple was built*]

A synagogue needs a cupboard, called an ark, for the Torah scroll(s), and an "eternal light" above it. The ark is usually on the wall facing Jerusalem.

1 ▶ *Look at the photographs of the open arks and discuss the differences.*

The Ark on the left is in Britain and has Ashkenazi style scrolls, with soft fabric covers and detachable silverware.
The Ark on the right is in India and has Sefardi style scrolls which are wooden or metal caskets.

Jews can pray anywhere and at any time but think that it is better to pray together. Every day there are three services: evening, morning and afternoon. There is an extra service on Shabbat and festivals, after the morning service. Most prayers are thanks and praise for God but some ask God to give or do something for the community or the world.

Rabbi Mendel of Kotsk lived in the early nineteenth century. One day a man came to him and said, "I am very poor. Please pray that I might be able to earn a decent living."

"Pray to God yourself," came the reply.

"But I don't know how to!" replied the man.

Rabbi Mendel's mouth dropped open in amazement. "You want a minor wish to come true," he said, "but you're not dealing with the major problem!"

" When we pray, we're talking to God in the presence of other people but we're also talking to each other in the presence of God. We say "you" to God and we say "we" about ourselves. Hardly any prayers say "I". People can put their own meaning into the prayers or even pray by themselves, but when we're together we're trying to pray as if we're all one person. "
[*Joyce*]

Religious Jews wear t'filin on their hand and before their eyes for morning prayers on weekdays. The small black boxes contain words of the Shema. The t'filin for the hand and arm has only one section inside: it symbolises that in their actions ("hand"), Jews should be united. The t'filin worn on the head, above the eyes, has four sections: it symbolises that in their thoughts ("head"), Jews may be very different and that there are many ways to "think Jewish".

Jews treat t'filin respectfully because they contain words of the Torah, written by hand on parchment by a qualified scribe. Once t'filin are made, they are only ever opened by a scribe to check that they are still perfect (except in this joke):

" One day, two children were fiddling with their father's t'filin. "I bet there's nothing inside. No one ever looks so what would be the point?" one of them said. "Scribes don't cheat!" said the other. But they were eaten up with curiosity and so they carefully unpicked the stitching round the edge to see. Inside was a tiny piece of rolled-up parchment. "It probably hasn't got anything written on it," said the first. "It must have!" said the other. They became even more curious and carefully unrolled the parchment to see. It read: "Help! I'm imprisoned in a t'filin factory!" "

"Love the Lord your God with all your heart, all your soul and all your might. These words that I command you today shall be upon your heart . . . Hold fast to them as a sign on your hand and let them be as reminders before your eyes." (part of the Shema prayer).
A t'filin stand in a Jerusalem street when men can stop and pray.

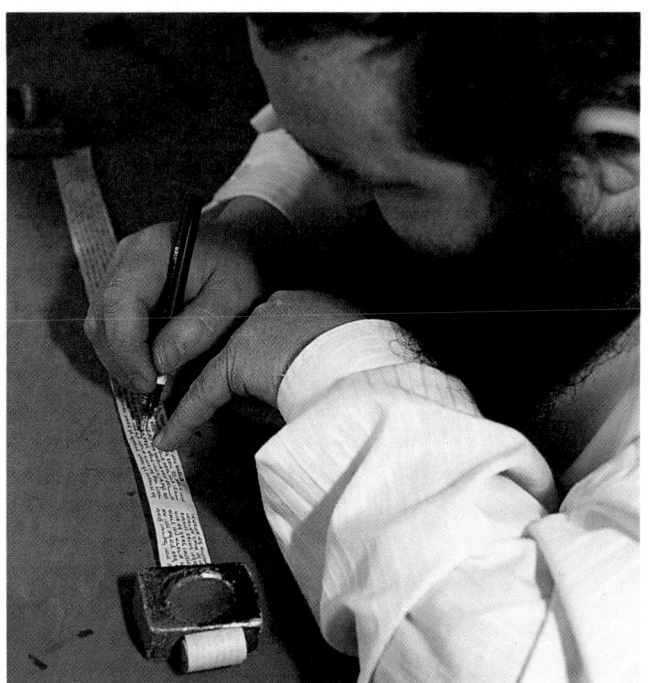

A scribe writing a piece of t'filin on parchment.

2 *Compare the ideas in this joke with the ideas of kissing prayer books and burying scrolls (see page 26). Is there a contradiction? Or are they saying the same thing?*

"Prayer, repentance and good deeds"

Rosh Hashanah and Yom Kippur fall in the autumn. The ark curtain and the covers of the Torah scrolls are usually white and some Jews wear white clothes. Red is the colour of sin and white is the colour of purity. It is a time of very intense prayer when Jews look back on the year that has gone and prepare for the coming year. They ask anyone they have hurt to forgive them and they try to make up for it in any way they can. Then they ask forgiveness from God and try to lead better lives.

The photograph shows a shofar being blown. The shofar is probably the world's oldest instrument. It has a haunting and piercing but mellow sound. It has the effect of "waking" Jews up to prayer, returning and charity, which are the themes of Rosh Hashanah and Yom Kippur. It is blown every day in the month before Rosh Hashanah, on Rosh Hashanah itself and at the end of Yom Kippur.

A man in white clothing, blowing a shofar.

A parent and a child are travelling together and pass a forest. The child stops and plays in the trees but after a while the parent says, "We must be on our way again. I'll start walking along the road and keep calling your name so that you can tell I'm still near. But when you can't hear my voice, you'll know that you'll soon be lost – and you must run with all your might to find me!"

 1 Create a picture, story or role-play about someone who has lost something very precious. What does it mean to them, why are they desperate for it and how do they go about finding it?

Hiding and seeking are very strong Jewish images and Jews sense that God is in hiding, waiting to be found. For many Jews, Rosh Hashanah and Yom Kippur are times when Jews feel that they have "lost" God and must "find" God again – when they feel closest to God. In this parable, the journey is an image of our lives, the parent is an image of God and the child is an image of each of us:

2 (a) Why does the parent leave the child alone in the forest for a while – and then keep calling out? How will the child be able to find the parent when he or she can't hear the parent's voice?

b) What is the parable saying about life, and about the relationship between God and people?

> ❝ Yom Kippur, the Day for Atonement, is a day of fasting and confession when we pray for forgiveness and promise ourselves that we'll be better in the future. But before that, we must do what we can to put right whatever's wrong in our lives, say sorry to people we have hurt and make it up to them. We can't have religion instead of justice because we believe the way we behave matters deeply to God. We say that on Yom Kippur we can make up for wrongs we have done to God but we can only make up for wrongs we have done to other people if we make peace with them. ❞
> [Elka]

3 ▸ Which hurts you more – hurting someone else or being hurt by someone else? Which do you find easier – forgiving someone else or forgiving yourself? Is it important to show that we are sorry in a practical way, such as by mending something we have broken, paying back something we have taken or making it up in some other way?

4 (a) The book of Jonah (in the Bible) is read on Yom Kippur. Read and talk about the story.
(b) What part of the narrative is shown in the sculpture in the photograph?
(c) How is the story linked with the themes of Yom Kippur?

The Ashamnu (meaning "We have abused") prayer is recited several times during Yom Kippur. The initial letters of the words make an alphabetical Hebrew acrostic, so it is easy to remember. Because the alphabet gives it a definite beginning and end, it reminds Jews that it is good to confess but not good to go on and on confessing. This English version cleverly uses the English alphabet:

We have **a**bused and **b**etrayed. We are **c**ruel. We have **d**estroyed and **e**mbittered other people's lives. We were **f**alse to ourselves. We have **g**ossiped about others and **h**ated them. We have **i**nsulted and **j**eered. We have **k**illed. We have **l**ied. We have **m**isled others and **n**eglected them. We were **o**bstinate. We have **p**erverted and **q**uarrelled. We have **r**obbed and **s**tolen. We have **t**ransgressed through **u**nkindness. We have been both **v**iolent and **w**eak. We have practised e**x**tortion. We have **y**ielded to wrong desires. Our **z**eal was misplaced.

A metal sculpture showing Jonah in the belly of the fish. The sculpture stands in the garden of the Museum of Biblical Art in Safed, Israel.

5 ▸ Can you write a statement, based on the English alphabet, for all the good things 'we' have done? Scan a dictionary if it helps.

"*In every generation*"

This unit is about birth and babies in the Jewish tradition.

The picture on the left shows an Orthodox family on an outing in London.

The picture on the right shows baby Moses being found. The ruler of ancient Egypt was trying to get rid of the Jews by killing the baby boys but Moses' mother had hidden him in the river to save him. Babies are Jewish if their mother is Jewish.

" Before a child is born, a light is held with which it can see from one end of the world to the other – and it knows the whole of the Torah. But at the moment of birth, an angel touches the baby on the lips and it forgets it all. So all our lives are spent remembering what we once knew. "
[*an ancient Jewish "explanation" as to why we have a "dip" between our lips and our nose!*]

1 *Talk about the quotation above. Do you ever have the feeling that you know something but do not know how you know it – or have you ever heard of someone who does? How can you explain this?*

A baby is a symbol of new life and a sign of hope for the future. Every Jewish baby is a person in its own right but also helps the Jewish people to survive. In the past, Jewish families were large, and traditional Jewish couples today still want to have lots of children.

> " Leah and Abe are Orthodox Jews who live in Jerusalem. Both of them go out to work and they have thirteen children. It is a happy and caring family, everybody pulls together and there is a great sense of togetherness at meal times and in family activities. I once asked them how they managed – and what the secret was. They replied, "The children keep each other happy. The more there are, the happier it is!" "
> [*Angela*]

> During the Holocaust, about a third of the world Jewish population was killed by the Nazis. I think that the generations who live after the Shoah must try to strengthen Jewish numbers. Of course, there's a big difference between quality and quantity but **sometimes quantity is also a quality.** "
> [*Rabbi Hugo Gryn*]

 Read what Rabbi Hugo Gryn says. What does the phrase that is in bold mean?

Names

Outside Israel, Jewish parents give their babies a Hebrew name as well as an "everyday" one, but sometimes it may be the same name, perhaps in a slightly different form; for example, a girl might be called Rebecca in English and Rivka in Hebrew. Sometimes the parents choose an "everyday" name which has a similar meaning to the Hebrew name but appears to be different. For example, a boy who has a French-speaking mother and an English-speaking father, has the "everyday" French name Olivier – which means an olive tree – and a Hebrew name Noah. The connection is through the Bible story of Noah, the flood, the ark, the dove and the olive branch.

Hebrew names are always "so-and-so the son/daughter of (father's name)". For example, Ruth, the daughter of Abraham. Nowadays, some Jews have both their mother's and their father's name in their name; for example, Emanuel, the son of Nathan and Ester. Outside Israel, Jews are usually only called by their Hebrew names if they are called to read or say the blessings for the Torah, on their wedding contract, and at their funeral and on their tombstone. Sefardi parents usually name their children after living relatives. Ashkenazi parents usually name their children after dead relatives.

 Does your name have a meaning? Who or what are you named after, and who gave you that name? How are names for babies chosen in your family? How do you feel when someone gets your name wrong? Do you ever want to change your name?

SIXTEEN

"Blessed is the one who comes in the name of God"

This unit is about the ways that Jews welcome a new-born baby in the family and in the community.

   God said to Abraham, "This is my covenant which you shall keep, between me and you and your children after you; every male among you shall be circumcised."
[*Genesis 17:10*]

The Lord your God will circumcise your heart, and the heart of your children, to love the Lord your God, with all your heart and with all your soul, that you may live. "
[*Deuteronomy 30:6*]

The baby's aunt bringing him in for his brit milah.

When a Jewish baby boy is eight days old, there is a ceremony called brit milah (or "brit" for short), which roughly means the covenant of cutting. It is a family event and a time to celebrate. The brit is a simple act of circumcising (cutting off) the foreskin of the baby's penis. It dates from the time of Abraham and the early Hebrews, about 2000 BCE. It is a sign for ever that the baby is a Jew and a sign for the whole Jewish people that there is a covenant, a special promise, between them and God.

    John Cohen is a mohel (someone who carries out a circumcision) and also a doctor. He says:

   The key players are the father, the grandfather and, of course, the baby. I see the mother and baby a few days after birth to be sure the baby is well. If he isn't, I postpone the brit. Otherwise, it happens on the eighth day. Usually the brit is in the home, and family and friends gather for the occasion. Before I start, I say a few words about the meaning of the brit and how it brings the baby into the covenant that God made with Abraham. The brit is a way of connecting this child with the long line of Jews since Abraham. The actual circumcision doesn't last very long and it's a lovely service. I understand that the mother, especially, may be anxious about the brit. The baby is so tiny and she feels especially close and protective at this time. But babies feel pain less at this age than when they're older. The baby has a drop of wine and a good feed from his mother. I love this work. It's a beautiful mitzvah. "

Dr. John Cohen holding the baby up as everyone says, "Blessed is the one who comes in the name of God."

 1

(a) *Why does a mohel postpone the brit if the baby is unwell? What Jewish value is shown here? (The clue is on page 21.)*

(b) *Why is it important for the father to be especially involved in the brit?*

(c) *Look at the quotation from Deuteronomy 30:6. What do you think "circumcise your heart" means?*

Community welcome

The parents usually take their baby to synagogue soon after birth to announce his or her name, to give thanks for the baby and to give members of the community a chance to welcome their youngest member. This is part of a prayer of thanks said by a mother for her baby daughter:

> Father of all mankind and source of life . . . I thank you for my life and for the life of my child, for you renew the wonder of creation. As she grows in body and in mind, **may the law of truth be found on her lips and the love of justice in her heart. May she be a blessing to those around her and bring honour to Israel in the sight of all humanity.**

 2

(a) *Read carefully and talk about the parts of the mother's prayer that are in bold print. What hopes for the child is the mother expressing?*

(b) *Millions of babies are being born right now. Imagine the situation one of them is being born into. What do you hope for that baby? What will the baby most need in life? What qualities do you hope it will have? What kind of world do you want it to grow up in? Write your thoughts and hopes as a prayer, a poem or in any other form.*

(c) *Why do you think Jews have different ways of celebrating the birth of girls and boys? What does this tell us about the different way that men and boys, and women and girls are seen in the Jewish tradition? Look back to pages 16–17.*

"Today I am a man . . . woman"

This unit is about coming of age in the Jewish tradition – about a boy becoming Bar Mitzvah and a girl becoming Bat Mitzvah.

1 (a) At what age do you think someone becomes an adult and responsible for their own actions? Is it the same for girls and boys? Does everybody grow up at the same time?

(b) How would you like to celebrate becoming an adult?

A Bar Mitzvah at the Western Wall in Jerusalem, reading from a Sefardi scroll. He is wearing t'filin (see page 29) because the Torah reading is on a weekday – either Monday or Thursday.

Jewish law says that a boy is an adult at the age of thirteen and a girl at the age of twelve. For many centuries, this turning-point has been marked for a boy by calling him to read the Torah or lead prayers in the service. He is called Bar Mitzvah, son of the commandment. Usually there is a celebration in the family and the community.

For many young people, growing up is about trying to be independent. In wanting to be an individual, they sometimes react against what the older generation expects of them. The theme of independence and individuality comes out in this story of a Jewish community in Poland about 200 years ago. When the beloved rabbi died, his son was chosen to take his place. He had different ideas and ways from his father and people complained that he was trying to change things. "You're not like your father!" they moaned. "Yes, I am," he replied. "I'm *exactly* like my father. My *father* never copied anyone – and *I* never copy anyone!"

2 In what ways do you and other teenagers you know show their independence and individuality? Who do they choose to copy – and how and why do they copy them? Can you copy someone else and still be an individual?

In this century, many families have wanted to mark a girl's coming of age. In traditional congregations, this has happened in various ways but the most common is for a group of girls to study together for about a year and then to have a special service where they read poetry and give a short talk, followed by a family or community celebration. In Progressive congregations, boys and girls celebrate coming of age in exactly the same way, usually when both are aged thirteen. The girl is called Bat Mitzvah, daughter of the commandment.

When Ester celebrated becoming Bat Mitzvah, she read this from the prayer book, in front of the congregation:

A proud grandmother of the Bat Mitzvah, tenderly leaning forward to kiss her.

"In the presence of my teachers, the leaders and the members of **this holy congregation**, I now prepare to take upon myself **the duties which are binding on all the family of Israel**. I ask their help in the years that lie ahead to strengthen my loyalty and devotion so that I may grow in charity and good deeds. I think also of **those who have gone before me**, who through all the troubles of the world preserved this heritage of holiness and goodness, so that I should enter into it now. May I be a true Bat Mitzvah, a daughter of the commandment, **taking my place in the community of Israel**, accepting its responsibilities, rejoicing in its blessing. May I be **a witness to the living God** and His goodness, and the tradition that lives within me . . ."

3 (a) *The prayer said by a boy who is celebrating becoming Bar Mitzvah is very similar to the prayer Ester read out. What would be different?*

(b) *Look at each of the sentences that are in bold print. Choose one and create a poem, story or picture to express what it means.*

4 *Write a speech for a person of your age to celebrate some important turning-point in their life as a young adult. It could be "spoken" by the person celebrating, with them saying what kind of adult they would like to be, or it could be spoken for them by a friend or relative who expresses hopes and good wishes for their adult life.*

5 *What kind of role models do you think young people need today?*

"*A seal upon your heart*"

This unit is about Jewish views on marriage.

The Song of Songs is a book in the Bible. It is a love poem, where the man and the woman declare their love for each other in romantic and passionate words. Jews also see it as a poem about the deep love between God and Israel. This picture appears in an illustrated copy of the Song of Songs *published in Jerusalem in 1923.*

> " When a soul is sent down from heaven, it is both male and female. The male part enters the male child and the female part enters the female child. When they are united in marriage, this is true mating."
> [*a saying from the Zohar, a thirteenth-century mystical work*]
>
> From every human being, there rises a light that reaches straight to heaven. When two souls, that are destined to be together, find each other, their streams of light flow together and a single brighter light goes forth from their united being. "
> [*Baal Shem Tov*]

 1   (a) Talk about the meaning of the two quotations above.
(b) Choose one and represent its meaning in art form, such as a picture or model, or create a "human sculpture" of bodies – or as the basis for a wedding invitation or card.

מי יתנך כאח לי יונק שדי אמי אמצאך בחוץ אשקך גם לא יבוזו לי: אנהגך אביאך
אל בית אמי תלמדני אשקך מיין הרקה מעסיס רמוני: שמאלו תחת ראשי וימינו
תחבקני: השבעתי אתכם בנות ירושלם מה תעירו ומה תעררו את האהבה עד שתחפץ

This is a story set in the time of the Roman empire:

Roman noblewoman   *What has your God been doing since creating the world?*
Rabbi Yose bar Halafta   *The Holy One, blessed be he, is busy making marriages.*

Roman noblewoman   *What kind of occupation is that? I have male and female slaves and could marry them all off in less than an hour!*
Rabbi Yose bar Halafta   *It might seem simple to you but every marriage is as difficult for the Holy One, blessed be he, as dividing the Red Sea.*

The following morning, in the Roman noblewoman's home.

Roman noblewoman   *Rabbi, last night I took a thousand male slaves and a thousand female slaves, placed them in two rows and married them to each other. This morning every single one of them was injured . . . One had a wounded head, one had a bruised eye, one had a fractured arm, one had a broken foot . . . You can imagine what must have happened in the night! They complained that they did not want to be married to the one I gave them!*
Rabbi Yose bar Halafta   *The Torah is true and wonderful!*

 (a) *What did happen in the night in the noblewoman's home?*
(b) *What does "dividing the Red Sea" refer to? (Read Exodus 14:21–22).*
(c) *Why is it harder to make a suitable match than to divide the Red Sea?*
(d) *Why did Rabbi Yose bar Halafta conclude that the "Torah is true and wonderful"?*

 What qualities would you look for in a marriage partner? Do you think someone of the opposite sex would look for the same qualities in you? If your family chose a marriage partner for you, would they look for the same qualities as you?

Traditionally, Jewish communities had matchmakers who arranged meetings between eligible Jewish men and women. It was a very important and honourable role, and it was not thought shameful for single people and their families to ask a matchmaker's help. Today, most single Jewish people choose their own partners but there are Jewish "dating agencies" and many synagogues and organisations hold functions for single people.

NINETEEN

"Be holy to me"

This unit is about the Jewish wedding ceremony.

A Jewish wedding is called "huppah and kiddushin". Kiddushin means "holiness" – marriage is a special relationship and the couple are set aside and holy for each other. The huppah is the canopy under which the couple, usually with their parents, stand. It symbolises the openness of their home. The wedding can be held anywhere and the best place is outside, open to the sky. British weather makes it difficult to plan for an outdoor wedding so it is usually held in a synagogue.

The ring, the words spoken by the man to the woman, the ketubah (wedding contract) and the two witnesses show that the wedding is an agreement between the two people. The ring must belong to the man first. The woman extends the index finger of her right hand and the man places the ring on it, saying, "Be holy to me according to the law of Moses and of Israel." The two witnesses must make sure that this has happened. Traditionally, the woman does not give a man a ring and does not reply: by accepting the ring, she shows that she is willing to marry him. Some Jewish women today also give the man a ring and say similar words. At Progressive weddings, both men and women speak their pledge and the words of the ketubah reflect this.

The ketubah, which means writing, is a record of what happened and a Jewish legal document. It is given by the man to the woman and remains her possession. It states what the man's responsibilities are to her. If the couple divorce at any time, the ketubah protects the woman's rights to maintenance. Many ketubot (plural) are beautifully illustrated with symbols and motifs that reflect the meaning of the wedding.

A wedding under a huppah. The Hebrew in the middle is the beginning of the phrase "Blessed is the one who comes in the name of God." The Hebrew over the two crowns says "Mazal Tov!" - Good luck" - which is what everyone calls out at the end of the service.

(a) Look at the photograph of the ketubah. What do the symbols of the ketubah represent?

(b) What responsibilities do you think a husband should have towards his wife and what responsibilities should a wife have towards her husband?

(c) Design a wedding contract or agreement between the wife and husband, with symbols representing the feelings and values they have.

Other parts of the wedding service reflect "kiddushin" and make it a beautiful occasion as well as a legal act. The couple drink twice from a cup of wine and, usually, the rabbi or a close friend speaks to the couple and the guests about marriage and family life. A song of Seven Blessings is sung near the end of the wedding service.

At the very end of the wedding, it is a custom for the man to smash a glass with his foot. This symbolises many things: a traditional interpretation is that it recalls the destruction of the ancient Jewish temple and the idea that, even when we are most happy, there is a touch of sadness in our lives.

Traditionally, while the guests started the celebrations after the wedding, the couple spent time together and alone. This is called "yihud", which means "union", and it shows that the relationship between the husband and wife is the most important thing about a wedding. Yihud used to last for hours or days and would give the couple the chance to make love, with the witnesses guarding their room so that they would be undisturbed. Today, most couples do not practice yihud in this way, though sometimes they have a few moments together in private.

This ketubah (wedding contract) is the in the shape of a huppah. It was specially created by Gordon Charatan.

The traditional chair dance at the wedding party . . . A happy bride, with women family members and guests dancing in a circle round her. In the background, her husband is surrounded by men dancing round him. Soon their chairs will be lifted high and they will symbolically be joined by each holding the end of a piece of white cloth.

2 *Why do men and women play different roles in the traditional wedding service? Do you think that any of the changes that some Jews make today affect the relationship between the couple?*

3 *As in many other traditions, someone who knows the couple well usually makes a speech at the wedding party. What thoughts, advice and good wishes would you want to give to someone you know who was getting married? You could write this as a speech.*

Have a good cry!

This unit is about the ways Jews view death and how they react to it.

" Days are scrolls. Write on them what you want to be remembered.
[*Bachya ibn Pakuda, 1050 –1120*]

In the world to come, we will have to give account of all the good things we could have enjoyed and did not.
[*a saying of Rav, a third-century rabbi*]

Live one life at a time. "
[*Jewish folk saying*]

1 (a) *Make one of these sayings into a card suitable for someone whose loved one has died.*
(b) *What would you like to be remembered for?*

2 (a) *What is "a good cry" and how does it help?*
(b) *Why is showing feelings respect for the dead?*
(c) *If you experienced the death of someone you loved or know someone who has, try to remember your or their feelings at the time. Have these feelings changed over time? What helped – or didn't help – you or them to grieve well? How did you or they show respect for the dead?*

" Have a good cry. It's no good trying to be brave. You've got your feelings and they're normal. If you don't let them out now, they'll come out later. Anyway, you owe it to him to show that you miss him. It's respect for the dead and it's a mitzvah. "
[*David and Fanny, to a cousin, on the day of a relative's funeral*]

Manny said this to his only grandchild, in hospital just before he died: "Another patient asked me what Jews believe about death and after that. I said we don't know – and I think he was shocked. I said this life is enough, without another life. You can't be sure what will happen and you can't do anything about it so why worry? Maybe my old body will come back to life . . . maybe I'll float like a spirit and meet up with Alice's [his wife's] spirit . . . maybe I'll wait for the world to end and the Messiah to come and then we'll all live again for ever . . . But if I do live on, it will be in you. You're all I have and that's all I need."

Russian Jewish women laying wreaths to remember and honour the dead at the site where thousands of Jews were massacred.

3 *Talk about what Manny said. Are you "shocked" by anything? Do you think people are helped by believing in something very definite about the afterlife? How do people "live on" in this life?*

When Jews die, they usually leave their money and property to their family or a charity in their will. Some also leave an "ethical will" – a legacy of their ideas and ideals which may be in what they say before they die or in something they write and which is read after they die. This "Ethical Will and Testament to His Grandchildren, and to Children Everywhere" was written by an American Jew:

I leave to you not everything I never had, but everything I had in my lifetime: a good family, respect for learning, compassion for my fellowman, and some four-letter words for all occasions: words like "help", "give", "care", "feel" and "love". Love is easier to recommend than to define. I can tell you only that like those who came before you, you will surely know when love ain't; you will also know when mercy ain't and brotherhood ain't. The millennium will come when all the "ain'ts" shall have become "ises" and all the "ises" shall be for all, even for those you don't like. Finally, I leave you the years I should like to have lived so that I might possibly see whether *your* generation will bring more love and peace to the world than ours did. I not only hope that you will. I pray that you will.
(Grandpa Sam Levenson)

4 *What do you wish for the world that you would like to see in your lifetime and leave after you have died? You could write this as an ethical will to your generation or a younger generation.*

A symbolic fire burning at the site of rabbis' tombs in Tiveriya (Tiberius), Israel.

Graves on the Mount of Olives, just outside the Old City of Jerusalem. In Jewish legends, the graves of the dead will open in the Last Days and the dead will rise: it is said that this will begin on the Mount of Olives when the Messiah appears (see pages 56 - 57).

43

*T*he house of life

This unit is about Jewish funerals and how Jews mourn their dead.

> May the Lord comfort and sustain you among the other mourners for Zion and Jerusalem.
> [*from the prayer book*]

Jewish mourning customs help people grieve freely and it is normal for men, women and children to cry openly. Mourners are excused normal duties so that they can concentrate on grieving. Relatives and friends do what they need and help them talk about their feelings. Synagogues make the funeral arrangements. For centuries, Jewish communities have had groups of volunteers who care for the dead and comfort the mourners. Their name – "hevra kadishah", holy society – shows how much this is valued.

When someone knows they are dying, they try to make a confession and say the Shema. If they cannot, someone else may say the Shema for them. When they die, they are not left alone and it is usual to light a candle near their head. Jewish funerals usually take place very soon afterwards, partly out of respect for the dead and partly to help the mourners grieve. A Jewish funeral is called a "l'vayah", which means "accompanying" as Jews are accompanying the dead person to their grave. The dead person is carefully washed and wrapped in a white shroud and men are also dressed in their tallit (prayer shawl). Most Jews are buried but some Progressive Jews choose to be cremated. Some communities place the body directly in the ground; others place it first in a coffin.

One of a series of paintings depicting the work of the hevra kadisha in Prague, by an unknown artist from 1780 onwards.

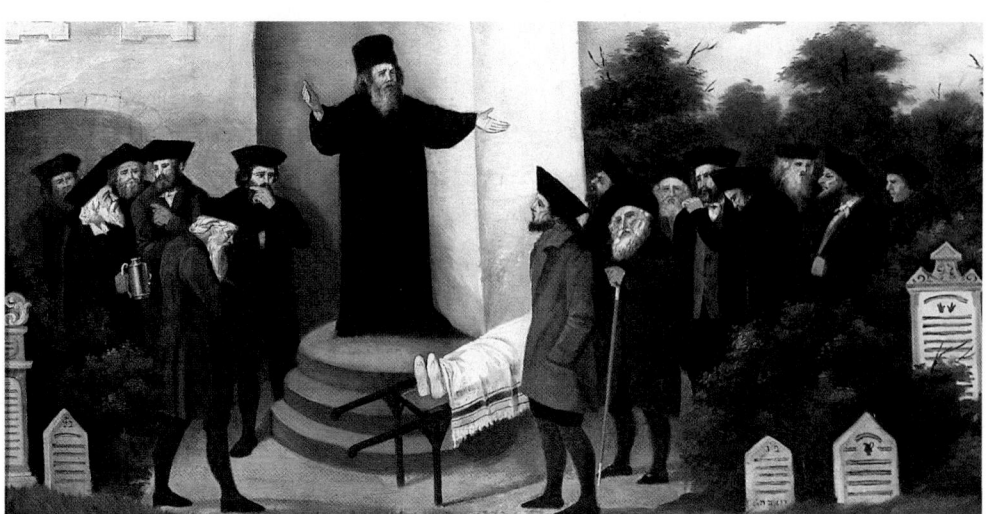

The Hebrew names for a cemetery are "house of life" or "eternal house". The words and actions in the funeral service help Jews to face the reality that someone they loved has died and will not return, but that life for others goes on. Jewish tradition knows that people need time to understand and accept that.

 1 *At Jewish funerals mourners throw some soil into the grave. Why do you think this is done?*

Several stages in mourning ease grief and the gradual return to life. The first is between death and the funeral. The first week after death is "shiva", meaning seven. There are no weddings or parties during shiva but people meet in the house of mourning for prayers, and to share happy memories and sad feelings. Mourners sit on low stools, as a sign of "low" feelings. Usually the rabbi, a relative or close friend talks about the dead person so that everyone can remember good things about them. During shiva, mourners do not go to work or school.

After shiva and in the rest of the thirty days after death, life slowly returns to normal, mourners go back to work or school, and weddings in the family can take place. Every day for a year, close mourners recite the kaddish, the memorial prayer which does not mention death at all but praises God as the giver of life. On the anniversary of someone's death, close relatives light a memorial candle and say, "The memory of the righteous is as a blessing." Within a year of the burial, the gravestone is set. Most have a simple design and wording. When visiting a grave, it is a custom to place a small stone there. Ashkenazi gravestones are laid either horizontally or vertically. Sefardi gravestones are always laid horizontally to show that, in death, everyone is equal.

2 *How do Jewish mourning practices show respect for the dead? Do you think they help people to grieve and to go on living after their loved ones have died?*

> ❝ I only understood why there's a tap in the cemetery grounds and why we wash our hands before we leave, when I went to a Jewish funeral for the first time. I had no soil on my hands so it wasn't something physical. But somehow death soils or spoils us and we need to be fresh again for our own life. As I washed my hands, I felt I was leaving death in the cemetery – where it belongs – and not carrying it back into my life. It wasn't sudden but I had to return to the world of living people. Washing my hands helped me a lot. ❞
> [Elka]

The tomb of The Rambam in Tiveriya (Tiberius), Israel. 'The Rambam' is the Hebrew title of Rabbi Moses Maimonides (see page 7).

The time of the whirlwind

This unit is about the Jewish experience of the Shoah (Holocaust) in the 1930s and 1940s.

Jews lived in Europe for almost 2000 years. In many countries, Christians persecuted and often killed them, because they believed that Jews killed Jesus and should be punished for it. Jews were often blamed for anything that went wrong. In some countries, Jews had to live in walled areas, called ghettos.

In 1933, soon after the Nazi party came to power in Germany, the Nazis began passing many laws against Jews – forbidding them to run a business, go out at night . . . Jews had to wear a yellow star so that they could be identified. The Nazis were popular partly because they hated the Jews and blamed them for the trouble the country was in.

The Nazis conquered other countries and spread the idea that the Jews and other "inferior races" should be exterminated. Between 1939 and 1945 they killed about 6,000,000 Jews – including about 1,500,000 babies or children. The Nazis became "better" at killing people quickly. They had concentration camps and death camps, with gas chambers, crematoria and mass graves. This period and these events are called the Holocaust, which means "burnt offering". Most Jews call it the "Shoah", the Hebrew word for whirlwind.

1 *Why do you think that Jews prefer to use a Hebrew word – and why that particular word?*

'The Faces of Learning' – boys in a Jewish school, 1937. The photographer, Roman Vishniac, took great risks to record Jewish life in Eastern Europe. His collection is called 'A Vanished World'.

The word "holocaust" is sometimes used for other massacres. For many Jews, though, the Shoah is different from other holocausts because:

- six million was about one-third of all the Jews alive at the time;
- the Nazis killed most Jews in Europe which was the heart of the Jewish world then;
- the Shoah was not just one event but part of a long history of hatred against the Jews;
- even when they were losing the war, the Nazis went on killing Jews instead of concentrating on winning the war;
- the Nazis aimed to kill all Jews *everywhere*.

One of the concentration camps was in Terezin (or Teresienstadt) which is now in the Czech Republic. From there, many Jews were taken to death camps. When news of concentration camps reached the outside world, the International Red Cross asked to inspect the camps. They were taken to Terezin which looked a bit like an ordinary town so they never got a true idea of the real horrors of such places. Terezin was really the "nicest" of the concentration camps: as people arrived, there was an orchestra playing music and some people could get paper. They wrote or drew about their life in the camp, about their life before they were taken away to the camp, and about their hopes for the future.

 Why do you think it was important for Jews in the Shoah to write and draw if they could?

This modern painting appears in a haggadah, read at the seder, the Passover supper (see pages 14 - 15). The Hebrew in the picture says: "This promise has stood by our ancestors and ourselves." In the picture, there are images of concentration camps in the Sea of Reeds through which the ancient Jews escaped.

- *Why do you think the artist has combined these images?*

'Workers' – a painting by a prisoner in Mauthausen camp. The words on the gate mean 'Work makes free'.

Remember

This unit is about the way that Jews today respond to the Holocaust, and about the importance of witness, memory and hope.

Jews value memory very much. It connects them with their past, puts them in touch with good things, strengthens them to fight bad things and renews their hope. They believe that they do not heal by forgetting; but they heal by remembering.

In Jerusalem there is a museum and memorial to the Shoah called Yad V'Shem. In an avenue of trees, near the entrance, each tree has been planted in the name of a non-Jew who helped to save Jews – such as Oskar Schindler, a German who is now famous because of the book *Schindler's Ark* and the film *Schindler's List*. The trees are a way of saying thank you to them and showing that something has grown from

their action. Some Jews place stones at the foot of the trees, as they do when visiting a grave.

Every year on Yom HaShoah, Holocaust memorial day, there is a gathering in Hyde Park, in London. "Zog nit keynmol" is sung then – and at other times and places where the six million are remembered. It was composed in Yiddish, in one of the camps, and became the banner song of survival. In an English translation, the first line runs: "You must never say that you walk the final path . . ."

In the gardens of Yad V'Shem, a sculpture showing children huddled against Janusz Korczak who ran an orphanage in Warsaw, Poland. In 1942, the Nazis came to take the children - but not Korczak - to concentration camps. Yet he did not want the children to be alone, frightened and uncared for so he went with them. Korczak and the children were all murdered by the Nazis. Visitors have placed stones on the sculpture just as they would when visiting a Jewish grave.

Some sort of thought

When twelve-year-old Tamar and Shoshi, first attended a Yom HaShoah service in their synagogue, they said:

> ❝ It began with Mum singing *The Yellow Butterfly*, a poem written by a child in Terezin who wanted to be as free as the butterfly to fly away. We said the kaddish, a prayer for the dead and, between every few words, Dad read out loudly the name of a concentration or murder camp.
>
> The biggest community we know is our school, with 1000 pupils, and I can't imagine 6,000,000. When you think of all the grief when just one person dies and then multiply that by a number you can't even imagine . . .
>
> **Remembering is what keeps it alive. If you forget, there's no point in it happening. To remember it, you've got to experience some sort of thought about it. In the service, everyone was together – maybe feeling different things, but joined in a bond.** ❞

> " The Valley of Communities at Yad V'Shem is a maze of narrow paths, lined by tall slabs of stone. It gave me the feeling of a small, dense town – but with nobody living there. Each stone has the name of a region of Europe – and the names of communities that were destroyed in the Shoah. Some people light memorial candles by the stones – as they would in their home when someone had died. "
> [*Ester, 12*]

One of the 'streets' in the Valley of Communities. The writing on the wall says 'Prague'.

 1
(a) *What do you think Shoshi and Tamar mean by the parts that are in bold print? Have you ever thought or felt that?*
(b) *Start making six million dots on a large sheet of paper.*

Jews respond to the Holocaust by remembering the dead and valuing life, by struggling to stop such things happening ever again to anyone and also through humour. Laughter helps many people to cope with grief and maybe understand it better. Many Jews feel that God is with those who suffer and that God suffered in the Shoah – but that God laughs too. Humour helps Jews survive and strengthens their faith. This joke was told during the Shoah and survives:

A Jew who had no work and a family to support took a job in a circus. He had to put on a lion skin and wrestle with a tiger in a cage. He got down on all fours and did his best roar! As the tiger approached, he started to pray, "Hear O Israel, the Lord is our God ..." Surprisingly, the tiger continued, "The Lord is One!" – "I thought you were a *real* tiger!" the Jew exclaimed. "Ssh! Not so loud!" whispered the tiger. "D'you think you're the *only* Jew around here trying to make a decent living?!"

 2
(a) *Do you ever crack a joke when you are feeling miserable? How do you react when someone else tells a joke then? What does your reaction depend on?*
(b) *Why do you think that Jews told jokes during the Shoah?*

 3
(a) *Some people say the Holocaust was unsuccessful because it did not rid the world of all Jews. What would you say to them?*
(b) *Others say that the Holocaust never happened and is just a Jewish lie so that people will feel sorry for them. What would you say to them? Do you think Jews want people to feel sorry for them?*

A little piece of land

1 ▶ *Is it important to have your own "space" at home or in the classroom? Why? How would you feel and what would you do if your country was occupied or you were driven out of your homeland?*

Jews lived in the land of Israel until the first century. When the Romans occupied it, Jews were driven away and lived in exile, mainly in Europe and the Middle East. For centuries they longed to return. Their prayers are full of their hope to live again in the land of Israel, and to see Jerusalem, the capital, restored. Jerusalem was built on Mount Zion. Zion is a symbol of hope and stands for building God's kingdom in the world. From the end of the nineteenth century, Jews began to return to Israel. Some came because they were persecuted in the country where they were living. Others came because they wanted to build Jewish life again in the land.

Psalm 126 was written about 2500 years ago, when Jews were first exiled from Jerusalem – to the land of Babylon. They were able to return after seventy years. The psalm is sung at the beginning of thanksgiving for meals on Shabbat, festivals and other special occasions.

A man and a girl planting a sapling in The Forest of Peace, Jerusalem.

When the Lord brought back the captives to Zion
we felt as if in a dream.
Then our mouths were filled with laughter
and our tongues with song.

Even among the nations they said:
"What great things the Lord has done for them!"
Indeed the Lord has done great things with us!
How we rejoiced!

Lord, bring back those who cannot return,
like streams in a dry land;
that those who sow in tears
may reap in joy.

Though a man goes out weeping
carrying seed to sow;
he shall come back singing
carrying his sheaves.

2 In what way is Psalm 126 a song of thanks, a song of pleading and a song of hope? Why is it important for Jews to sing this song today? What situations and experiences might it refer to?

3 Use books and newspapers to research the history of modern Israel and construct a timeline from the Ottoman Empire to the present day. Include: the British Mandate; the United Nations partition; the War of Independence; the Six Day War; the peace treaty between Israel and Egypt; and the current discussions between Israeli and Palestinian leaders. Draw symbols or small sketches against each event on the line, to show what happened.

4 For a week, follow the news on television, radio or daily newspapers. Note every time Israel is mentioned and the sort of events that are covered. Why is there a lot of news coverage of Israel, compared with other very small countries? Does the coverage seem to be "for" or "against" Israel?

The Church of All Nations, in a garden that is thought to be the Garden of Gethsemane, near the Mount of Olives in Jerusalem. Israel is important to Christians as well as to Jews. Churches – like mosques – are safeguarded by law.

Declaration of the Establishment of the State of Israel

On 14 May 1948 the Declaration of the State of Israel was signed by David Ben Gurion, the first Prime Minister of Israel, and thirty-six world leaders. This is an extract from it:

> The State of Israel will be open for Jewish immigration and for the Ingathering of the Exiles; it will foster the development of the country for the benefit of all its inhabitants; it will be based on freedom, justice and peace as envisaged by the prophets of Israel; it will ensure complete equality of social and political rights to all its inhabitants, irrespective of religion, race or sex; it will safeguard the Holy Places of all religions, conscience, language, education and culture . . . We extend our hand to our neighbouring states and their peoples in an offer of peace and good neighbourliness, and appeal to them to establish bonds of cooperation and mutual help with the sovereign Jewish people settled in its own land.

Murals along a street in the town of Jericho which is now in the Palestinian administered region. The murals depict Arab leaders.

5 (a) Look at all the pictures of Israel in this book and match each one to a phrase in the Declaration.

(b) From your research of the media, can you find pictures or stories that show these "declarations" coming true and pictures or stories that show these "declarations" being ignored or denied?

The Good Fence

This unit is about the border between Israel and Lebanon, and what it tells us about the feelings that Jews in Israel have about peace, conflict and security.

The Israeli and the Lebanese flags at the Good Fence.

For several hundred years until the early part of this century, the Land of Israel and the surrounding Arab lands were part of the Ottoman (Turkish) Empire and there were no separate, independent countries within it. After the Ottoman Empire collapsed, the French and the British took control of the area, divided up the lands between them and created borders.

The town of Metulla is now on the northern border of Israel, in a thin strip surrounded by Lebanon on three sides. Terrorist groups often attack Metulla. In 1981 they fired over 2000 rockets in ten days. Yossi Goldberg is the Mayor and his family have lived there since the time of the Ottoman Empire. He says:

> **"** Israel has always been the Jewish people's home – the only country we've ever had. My grandparents came from Russia 100 years ago, fleeing attacks because they were Jewish. They wanted to live as a Jewish people and came to this little Jewish country.
>
> When my father was ten, gangs attacked the occupying French army who fled north, taking the Jews of Metulla with them. A Muslim doctor on the way gave my family shelter, food, money – everything! The Arab leader of Metulla was my grandfather's friend and gave the family protection on the dangerous journey home. **"**

In 1976, a Lebanese Christian refugee came to the border, asking them for shelter for 20,000 Christians. Yossi and the Jews of Metulla opened a gateway in the fence and took the wounded to Israeli hospitals. They piped water from Metulla to their town and built a clinic by the fence. Reporters called it the "Good Fence" and it is still known by that name. In time, friendship grew between the Jews of Metulla and the Lebanese people on the other side of the fence. Every day, over 1000 Lebanese cross to work, get medical treatment or visit relatives. There is a Jewish festival called Hanukah that comes around Christmas time. Every year, Yossi and his staff invite hundreds of Lebanese children to a party with Jewish children in Metulla. They have a wonderful day together.

Yossi personally wanted to thank the people who helped his family sixty years before so, in 1982, he invited the doctor's family to Metulla. They came for a meal and the Muslim doctor's son gave Yossi's father his own father's prayer beads. Yossi says:

The photo on the cover of this book shows Hanukah candles being lit on the fourth night of Hanukah. The girl is using the shammash (helper candle) to light the other candles. Then she will put the shammash in the middle candle-holder which is different from the rest. On the first night of Hanukah, one candle is lit and son on up to eight on the eighth night.

❝ That is a very symbolic gift. **There is a very special life here – with very special relationships!** All we have is this little piece of land where we can build a Jewish life, with a Jewish government. We never know *when* we'll be attacked but we know *that* we'll be attacked. What should we do – leave? **My father and I were born Palestinian Jews: no one can take us from this place!** Do you know what it means to open the border to the other side, where some dream of killing you and destroying your country? **But we can't close the border: that's the risk we take for the sake of peace and the chance of a normal life.** I see Metulla as the window of Israel. **Here you feel what it's like to sit on the border and walk the bridge between neighbours.** ❞

Jews and Christians meet at the Good Fence for a summer camp.

1 *Either: Imagine that you were present when the Muslim doctor's family came to visit Metulla. Write about it to a friend.*
Or: Imagine that you are a child who goes to the party at Hanukah and Christmas time. Write an entry about it in your diary.

2 *Read again what Yossi says about the special life in Metulla. What do you think the sentences in bold mean?*

3 *Do you think that the people of Metulla are right to stay there? Should they move to a safer part of Israel? Do you think the people of Metulla are right to keep the "Good Fence" open when there are still attacks from south Lebanon? Imagine that you are a reporter, interviewing a Jew who lives in Metulla and that you put these questions to him or her. Write a newspaper article, quoting what they might say.*

Neighbours and cousins

This unit is about the relationship between Jewish and Muslim neighbours in Jerusalem, and the feeling that Jews and Arabs are cousins.

Away from the big news events, there are also simple, everyday stories about cooperation and trust between the peoples of Israel. Many of them want to live together in peace and make deep and lasting friendships. This is a story that Angela was told:

> " For centuries, a Muslim Arab family and a Jewish family were neighbours in the Old City of Jerusalem. They shared a balcony and a courtyard where the children played together and older people sat and talked. The Jewish father was caretaker of the little synagogue next door.
>
> During the War of Independence in 1948, the Old City was occupied by Jordan and most of the Jewish population was either killed or fled. Before he and his family escaped, the synagogue caretaker closed the ark and entrusted the keys to his Arab neighbour. During the occupation, many Jewish sites of the Old City were destroyed or neglected – but the Arab family made the synagogue part of their home, taking care not to damage the scrolls and books.
>
> In 1967, surrounding Arab countries attacked Israel, but on the sixth day news came that Israeli forces were victorious and were entering the Old City. The Arab father grabbed the synagogue keys and rushed to meet them. He thrust them into a soldier's hand and said, "My family has looked after your synagogue for nineteen years. Now it's yours again!" The synagogue was restored and is now used regularly. "

Jews and Arabs in a market street near the 'room', in the Old City of Jerusalem.

Angela says, "In 1994, as the Arab father was telling the story in the street outside the house, the grandson of his Jewish friend happened to walk past – and they hugged each other like uncle and nephew!"

 (a) *Why do you think that the news about Israel never covers "happy" stories like this? Would people like to read or hear them?*

(b) *Write the story of the room as a newspaper article, with a headline and ideas for pictures, with captions.*

Isaac and Ishmael

Abraham lived about 4000 years ago. His Egyptian wife, Hagar, bore him a son, Ishmael. His Hebrew wife, Sarah, bore him a son, Isaac. Jews today believe that Jews and Muslims are descended from Abraham – through Sarah and Hagar – and are "cousins".

Abraham believed that he should sacrifice his son, Isaac, to God but that God sent an angel to stop it. Jews do not make human sacrifices. Muslims have a similar story but the son in their story is Ishmael.

 Read and talk about the story of the sacrifice of Isaac in Genesis 22.

The modern Israeli poet Shin Shalom writes in this poem as though he is Isaac to his "brother" Ishmael – as if they are both living today. He is sad about the trouble between their two peoples and hopes that it will soon end, because he feels that the two peoples are joined together in history:

Ishmael, my brother,
How long shall we fight each other?

My brother from times bygone,
My brother – Hagar's son,
My brother, the wandering one.

One angel was sent to us both,
One angel watched over our growth –
There is the wilderness, death threatening through thirst,
I, a sacrifice on the altar, Sarah's first.

Ishmael, my brother, hear my plea:
It was the angel who tied me to thee ...

Time is running out, put hatred to sleep.
Shoulder to shoulder, let's water our sheep.

A painting of Yitzhak Rabin, Prime Minister of Israel, and graffiti on a wall near the spot where he was assassinated in October 1995. The large Hebrew letters say 'We will remember!'

 (a) *What might Abraham make of the relationship between the descendants of Isaac and Ishmael today? Write a letter, as if from Abraham, to either or both groups.*

(b) *Write a poem or letter to someone that you have had an argument with or do not get on well with, suggesting that you make peace and become friends.*

TWENTY-SEVEN

"The end of days"

This unit is about Jewish beliefs about the Messiah and their hope for a perfect age.

> " I believe with perfect faith in the coming of the Messiah and, even though he is delayed, still I believe.
> [*Maimonides' "Thirteen Principles of Faith", twelfth century*]

> . . . if I look up into the heavens, I think that it will all come out right, that this cruelty too will end, and that peace and tranquillity will return again . . . "
> [*The Diary of Anne Frank, 15 July 1944*]

For centuries, Jews have believed that people, by themselves, cannot make the world perfect – only God can – and that one day God will send the Messiah to bring about an ideal world. "Messiah" means anointed. In the Bible, when someone was anointed, oil was poured on their head as a sign of special power. King David was anointed and was thought to be a great king: some of the images Jews have of the Messiah come from David.

Many legends tell that the prophet Elijah will announce the coming of the Messiah, who will ride into Jerusalem on a donkey, and then the graves will open and the dead will rise.

In one legend, Elijah appeared to a rabbi called Baruka in a market place. Rabbi Baruka asked him, "Will anyone in this market have a share in the world to come?" Elijah said, pointing, "These two!" Rabbi Baruka asked them, "What's your job?" They said, "We're clowns and comedians! We cheer people up. When we see people quarrelling, we try to make peace between them."

1 (a) *What does the occupation of these two people say about Jewish values?*

(b) *What signs might there be that the days of the Messiah had come?*

2 (a) *In several passages in the Bible, there are images of what the world will be like when the Messiah comes, or in "the last days". Read and talk about the images in these passages: Isaiah 11:1–9; Jeremiah 31:31–34; Ezekiel 37:1–10; Micah 4:1–7; Joel 2:28–29.*

(b) *Design a poster for a bedroom wall, using one of these images from the Bible or your own image of the end of the world.*

> ❝ Most of us today don't really think about the *Messiah* – but about the *days of the Messiah* and what life will be like then. We can *wait* for it to happen or we can help to *make* it happen. If we *all* tried to get on with each other and shared things more, wouldn't the world be better – and wouldn't that be enough? I'd settle for that as the days of the Messiah more than someone on a donkey! ❞
> [*Elka*]

A picture of Rabbi Menachem Shneerson, on the wall of a fruit juice and ice-cream kiosk in a Jerusalem street.

Often in history there have been people claiming to be the Messiah or whose followers claimed they were. The Orthodox Jewish leader Rabbi Menachem Shneerson died in New York in 1994. His death made the news because a small group of Jews heralded him as the Messiah.

> ❝ They say he was something special. He was very wise and comforting, and always knew what to say to help people. Jews who weren't really sure about being Jewish felt their lives change when they met him. He just *has* to be the Messiah – and the good times are coming!
> [*Baruh*]
>
> I don't know what they see in him. If he's the Messiah, why's nothing changed? Life goes on the same. He may have lots of followers but so do football players and pop stars. Anyway, it's not the first time people thought someone was the Messiah and they turned out not to be. When the Messiah comes, we'll all know it! ❞
> [*Orna*]

One woman praying and another slipping a 'message' into the Western Wall.

 What do these two views of Rabbi Menachem Shneerson say about Jewish ideas of the Messiah?

A dream of ice-cream

One December, in Jerusalem, a teacher told her class of six-year-olds, "You've all worked very hard this term. The festival of Hanukah's coming and we're having a special treat. We'll go to the Western Wall where some people put little messages between the cracks. You can all write something and put it in! Then we'll see them lighting the big hanukiyah and *then* we're going for ice-cream!"

When one of the girls got home after the trip, her older sister asked, "What did you put on your paper?"

"I put that I hoped there would be *chocolate* ice-cream!"

"You put what? You should have put that you hoped the Messiah would come soon and stay for ever, and that the world would be perfect . . . You wasted a big chance!"

"But the teacher said we could put whatever we wanted!"

 (a) Was the older girl right to criticise her younger sister?
(b) If you had the chance to write a wish or hope for the world, what would you say?

A Jew today

This unit is about three ways of being Jewish in the modern world.

In this book, you have "met" many Jews – and different Jewish views and ways of life. Jewish life is always changing, but important beliefs and values stay the same. "The Jewish community across the world and down the ages is like a spectrum of blending colours." (Ester, 13)

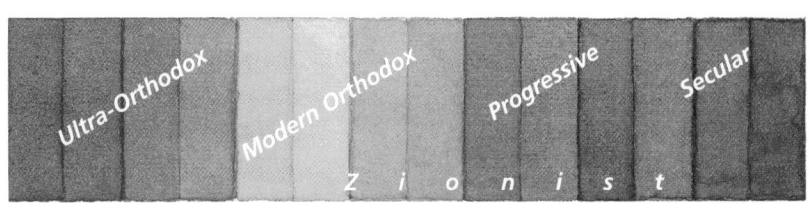

Ultra-Orthodox Jews, in fairly closed communities, observe the halaha (the body of traditional Jewish laws) completely and their way of life has changed very little over the centuries. Modern Orthodox Jews lead modern lives except where it is against the halaha. Progressive Jews think that Jewish life should take on the best ideas in the modern world. Secular Jews are not religious but keep some Jewish customs. Zionists believe in building up the Jewish people and the land of Israel: they can be modern Orthodox, Progressive or secular.

Joyce, Solomon and Marc have changed in the way they practise their religion, and the way they view life and what it means to be Jewish. Joyce grew up in an Orthodox American family. For a while she lived a secular life, and worked in Progressive summer camps and schools.

> " For me there are three ways to be *both* Jewish *and* modern: modern Orthodox, Progressive and Zionist. "
> [*Alice*]

> " It's an insult to God to pretend there's only one way to be an observant Jew. It's important for people to see that someone like me who looks like a normal human being can be Orthodox! The only way to make the Torah real is to live it – wherever and whenever you are. The whole beauty of the Torah is that you can belong in the world as it is: if the Torah couldn't be lived in any one time, it wouldn't be the Torah. I think of the Torah as an overcoat: I can shorten or lengthen it, or add a collar; I can take it with me wherever I go; and I can walk around in the cold air and always be warm. "
> [*Joyce*]

Joyce Klein in a Jerusalem street, in the new part of the city.

1 *Compare Joyce's image for the Torah with the images on page 9.*

Solomon's family is Sefardi, from Egypt. He grew up in Britain, and attended an Orthodox synagogue but now he, his wife and children are members of a Progressive synagogue.

Solomon Sananes and his family, who live in Leicestershire.

> " People have to do what they feel comfortable with in today's world. Antisemitism makes some Jewish communities closed and inward-looking. My parents taught us to respect Judaism but never to show it off. They taught us to respect other religions, too. But we shouldn't feel we're better or worse than anyone else. We have friends of different religions and we want our kids to be a real part of the world today. It's how you get on with other people that counts and you've got to have broad horizons. I'm extremely happy in a Progressive shul [Yiddish word for synagogue] and the service is very homely and peaceful to me. I can understand what's going on and really join in. I get 100 per cent fulfilment and what matters is what you feel in your heart. It's a direct relationship between me and above – and nobody else. "
> [*Solomon*]

2 *Sum up in your own words what matters most to Solomon about being Jewish.*

Marc came from the USA to live in Israel as a young man. His wife is Israeli and they have three children.

> " **Judaism isn't just a beautiful feeling. It's a way of living and giving something to society.** Any Jews who can think for themselves will have trouble accepting the halaha completely. The halaha today has to "speak" to today's human values and that means it has to change. Apart from the ultra-Orthodox, Jews outside Israel are all **part-time Jews**. Jewish survival depends on a strong Israel that cares about human values. If Jews really mean to **build God's kingdom here on earth**, they need their own society. **Israel is the one place in the world today where your whole life can be Jewish, where you can be both fully Jewish and fully human.** There are secular Jews who don't care about Jewish traditions and ultra-Orthodox Jews who don't care about questions of modern living. But for Jews who care about both, Israel is where they're connected. **Zionist is the Jewish way of being human.** "
> [*Marc*]

Marc Silverman, with his family, visiting the 'miniature town' model of ancient Jerusalem.

 3 (a) *What does Marc mean by the parts that are in bold print?*
(b) *What do Joyce, Solomon and Marc have in common?*

I am a Jew

This unit is about what it *means* to be a Jew.

Hugo Gryn grew up in a traditional Jewish family in the town of Berehovo, which is now in the Czech Republic. As a teenager, he was taken to a concentration camp where most of his family were killed. He became a rabbi and devoted his life's work to strengthening the Jewish people and to building bridges of peace and understanding between all peoples. One of his favourite parts of the Torah comes near the end: "I have put before you life and death, blessing and curse. Choose life so that you and your children may live." (Deuteronomy 30:19) As a young man, Hugo wrote this poem about being a modern Jew who is part of a long tradition:

Hugo, in his sixties, in the sukkah (see page 13) on the roof of his synagogue. He is holding a lulav and etrog, and talking to some of the children about Sukkot.

I am a Jew, the mortal Jew
who is immortal.

I am the ancient and the new.

I have prayed by the Jordan
And bathed in the Nile.
I wept at Babylon and rejoiced at Sinai.
I was reared through centuries by Fate
to a timeless chant.

I was loved for seconds,
Tolerated for seasons,
But loathed in the end.
I danced to the rhythm of race-hatred,
I performed to the mood of chance
To an audience of monarchs and gods.
When I pleased, I was applauded.
When I failed, I was chased
To find a new stage for my act.

A gambler for Life.

For life, naked life, any life,
With enough foul air to breathe.
I will bow, I will hush,
I will steal, I will lie,
I will beg, I will crawl,
For life, a bit of life.

Let it be misery,
Let it be treachery,
Let it be slavery,
Let it be hell,
But let it be life . . .

Notes

Jordan A river that runs from north to south in the Land of Israel, connecting the Kinneret (Sea of Galilee) with the Yam Ha'Melah (Dead Sea). In the Jewish Bible, crossing the Jordan is a symbol not only for entering the land but also for change and hope.

Nile A river in Egypt where the ancient Jews were slaves to the pharaohs until God set them free to be themselves and to live in their own land (approximately 1200 BCE).

Babylon An ancient city (in Iraq) to which Jews were deported in 586 BCE when the Babylonians sacked Jerusalem and destroyed the Temple. Babylon became a symbol for exile from the land and also, in a personal way, for a feeling of being "lost".

Sinai A mountain in the desert region between Egypt and the Land of Israel. There (perhaps about 1200 BCE) the Torah was revealed to the Jewish people through their leader, Moses. Sinai is a symbol of revelation, the many ways in which God "speaks" to people.

1 ▶ *Prepare and perform a group reading of the poem, adding background music if you wish or perform the poem as a dance or mime.*

2 ▶ *Using what you have learned about Judaism from this book and other sources, summarise the most important aspects of Judaism by:*
either creating a four-page leaflet about Judaism
or designing a poster with the caption "Judaism is . . ."

Hugo and Ester (see page 37) looking at the Torah one last time before she reads it the following day, when she celebrates becoming Bat Mitzvah.

Glossary

antisemitism   discrimination against, and persecution of, Jews

ark   cupboard containing Torah scrolls in synagogues – usually on wall facing Jerusalem

Ashkenazi   Jews originating in northern and eastern Europe

Bar Mitzvah   "son of the commandment": a boy who is 13 years old

Bat Mitzvah   "daughter of the commandment": a girl who is 12 years old or, in a Progressive community, 13

bimah   raised platform or reading desk in synagogues

brit milah   circumcision: marking a baby boy's entry into the covenant

halahah   the "h" in the middle is sounded in the throat – sometimes spelt "halachah"; the body of Jewish laws

hallah   the "h" at the beginning is sounded in the throat – sometimes spelt "challah"; bread of specially enriched dough for Shabbat and festivals

Hasidic   the "h" at the beginning is sounded in the throat – sometimes spelt "Chasidic"; literally meaning "pious"; the Hasidic movement began in Poland in the 18th century and emphasised purity of heart and joyous devotion to the Torah

havdalah   "separation": a ceremony to mark the end of Shabbat

Hebrew   the ancient and modern language which unifies the Jewish people; the language of the Torah and prayer books; the everyday language of Israel

hevrah kadishah   the "h" at the beginning is sounded in the throat – sometimes spelt "chevrah"; literally "holy society"; groups of volunteers who care for the dead and comfort the mourners

huppah   the "h" at the beginning is sounded in the throat – sometimes spelt "chuppah"; wedding canopy

Israel   the homeland of the Jewish people since ancient times; "the house of Israel" is a name for the Jewish people

Jerusalem   the capital city of Israel built on Mount Zion

kashrut   Jewish food laws: food that Jews may eat is called "kasher" or "kosher"

ketubah   a marriage document which the bridegroom gives to the bride

Messiah   "the anointed one" who, Jews believe, will one day bring a perfect age for everyone that will last for ever

mezuzah   a small box on doorposts of houses and rooms, containing a small piece of parchment with the words of the "Shema"

minyan   ten adult males making the minimum sized congregation for prayer, in Orthodox communities

mitzvah   plural: mitzvot; commandment

Orthodox   keeping the religion according to the halaha (law)

parev   or parve; food which is neither milk nor meat

Progressive   Reform or Liberal; interpreting traditional Judaism in the light of modern life; a form of Judaism which emphasises the teachings of the Bible more than the Talmud

rabbi   a Jewish religious teacher who may preach and act as a judge; most rabbis also do community work

secular   not religious; secular Jews identify with the Jewish people but do not observe Jewish practices

Sefardi   Jews originating in Spain, and other Mediterranean and Middle Eastern countries; Sefardi Jews spoke Ladino for centuries – a language similar to medieval Spanish

Shabbat   the Jewish Sabbath day, which lasts from sunset on Friday until sunset on Saturday

Shema   a passage from the Torah which is recited during evening and morning prayers, and, by some, in bed just before going to sleep. It begins, "Hear, O Israel, the Lord is our God. The Lord is One." The Shema is contained in the mezuzah and t'filin

shiva   literally "seven"; period of mourning, from the time of death for a week

Shoah   "whirlwind": the Nazi holocaust

shofar   ram's horn, blown on Rosh Hashanah (New Year) and daily throughout the month before to call Jews to spiritual awakening and repentance. It is also blown at the end of Yom Kippur (Day for Atonement) to announce that the fast is over

synagogue   the Jewish place of study, prayer and meeting; known as shul, bet hamidrash and bet knesset

tallit   prayer shawl; a striped and fringed rectangle of cloth, with tzitzit (bound and knotted fringes) at each corner

Talmud   "study": a collection of writings, completed in 500 CE, based on rabbis' discussions about right and wrong

Temple   the central place of Jewish worship from 1000 BCE to 70 CE, where priests offered sacrifices, in Jerusalem

t'filin   small boxes, worn on the head and the arm for prayers on weekday mornings, which contain extracts from the Torah (including the Shema) written on parchment by a trained scribe

Torah   the first five books of the Jewish Bible; Jewish teaching (ideas and values); Jewish way of life

tref   literally "torn"; food which is not kasher

Yiddish   language spoken by Ashkenazi Jews for centuries, based on medieval German and written in the Hebrew alphabet

Zionist   believing in the importance of the modern State of Israel, striving to improve the safety and welfare of Israel, and strengthening the society

Index

ANSWERS

Unit 2

The order of the captions is: 1C, 2D, 3G, 4A, 5B, 6F, 7H, 8E.

Unit 6

The themes and actions are matched as follows:
(a, C), (*b*, EF), (*c*, FG), (*d*, H), (*e*, AG), (*f*, C), (*g*, D), (*h*, F), (*i*, A–H).

Unit 8

3: Kasher: a, c, e. **Tref:** b, d.

4: Meat: c, e. **Milk:** b, g. **Parev:** a, d, f, h, i, j.

Unit 9

Meat: a, c, e.

Unit 12

4: *1* Torah scroll; silver; bells; synagogue.

2 bow; fringes.

3 Torah scroll.

4 lifted.

5 Torah; pointer; words; parchment.

6 Torah scroll; synagogue; ark.

Acknowledgements

I would like to thank many friends and relatives for contributing to this book, through their interesting and inspiring conversations, by allowing me to quote their words, by agreeing to be photographed and for their support, advice and encouragement. They include:

Abe Abramovitch, Leah Abramovitch, Rafi Bar Yaakov, Joanna Bower Ish-Horowicz, Shoshi Bower Ish-Horowicz, Tamar Bower Ish-Horowicz, Dr John Cohen, Samuel Gilmore, Elka Gluck, Ester Gluck, Manny Gluck, Yossi Goldberg, Rabbi Avraham Goldhar, Brad Goldhar, Yoheved Goldhar, the late Rabbi Hugo Gryn, Judith Ish-Horowicz, Dr Moshe Ish-Horowicz, Joyce Klein, Nathalie Lalonde, Clive Lawton, David Levene, Fanny Levene, Rachel Ouseley, Alice Quint, Solomon Sananes, Michael Shapiro, Amit Silverman, Marc Silverman, Orna Silverman, Rabbi Jacqueline Tabick, David Taylor, Rabbi Levy Weiman-Kelman and Rabbi Alexandra Wright.

Illustrations by:

Andy Hepworth p7; Sarah Jowsey pp6, 19, 58; Chris Molan p39; Colin MacNeil p16, 27; Martin Orme c/o Linda Rogers Associates pp15, 21.

The publishers would like to thank the following for permission to reproduce photographs:

Gordon Charaton: p41(top right); CIRCA Photo Library/ICOREC: p13(bottom right), CIRCA Photo Library/ICOREC/Barrie Searle: pp36, 40, 41(bottom right); Michael Dudley (Pessach Haggadah in Memory of the Holocaust): p47(bottom right); Guy Hall: pp4(top), 5, 9, 14, 18, 19, 20, 22, 23, 24, 25, 26, 30, 32, 34, 35, 37, 60, 61; Rupert Horrox: p38; IPPA Ltd: p53; Klub Bylych Wienzniow Mauthausen-Gusen (Association of Former Prisoners in Mauthusen-Gusen), Warsaw: p47(top); Network Photographers Ltd: p54; Solomon Sananes: p59(top); The Estate of Roman Vishniac (Mara Vishniac Kohn)/Institute of Contemporary History & Wiener Library Ltd: p46; Zidowské Museum (Jewish Museum), Prague: p44.

All other photographs are by Angela Wood.
Cover Photo: The Telegraph Colour Library/F.P.G./D Luria

With special thanks to the Akiva School, London and Carmelli's Bakery

OXFORD
UNIVERSITY PRESS
Great Clarendon Street, Oxford OX2 6DP

Oxford New York
Athens Auckland Bangkok Bogotá Buenos Aires
Calcutta Cape Town Chennai Dar es Salaam
Delhi Florence Hong Kong Istanbul Karachi
Kuala Lumpur Madrid Melbourne Mexico City
Mumbai Nairobi Paris São Paulo Singapore
Taipei Tokyo Toronto Warsaw

and associated companies in
Berlin Ibadan

Oxford is a trade mark of Oxford University Press
© Oxford University Press

First published in 1997
Reprinted 1998, 1999

ISBN 0 19 917252 8

A CIP catalogue record for this book is available from the British Library

Printed in China